THE ENDURING LINCOLN

LINCOLN

SESQUICENTENNIAL

LECTURES

AT THE

UNIVERSITY

OF ILLINOIS

ROY P. BASLER

T. HARRY WILLIAMS

DAVID DONALD

NORMAN A. GRAEBNER

EXHIBIT MATERIALS

SELECTED AND

DESCRIBED BY

LESLIE W. DUNLAP

UNIVERSITY

OF ILLINOIS

PRESS

URBANA

1959

THE ENDURING LINCOLN

EDITED BY
NORMAN A. GRAEBNER

PREFACE

This year a grateful nation again pays tribute to the memory of the man who above all others has come to symbolize America itself — its opportunities, its virtues, its sense of mission. One hundred and fifty years ago Abraham Lincoln was born in poverty on the frontier, and yet his career terminated in the highest office in the land. Throughout his life Lincoln revealed the homely virtues which Americans like to claim as their own — honesty, industry, a sense of humor, and a selfless devotion to right. Lincoln's intense devotion to the nation — its Constitution, its laws and traditions — prompted him to attribute a cosmic quality to American democracy. For him the country's special obligation to humanity lay in demonstrating ceaselessly the superiority of its institutions by the quality of its example.

But this sesquicentennial of Lincoln's birth is more than an exercise in respectful memory; it is a challenge to the intellect. Lincoln merits the nation's esteem not only because of the peculiar quality of his statesmanship, but also because of the timelessness of the precepts which guided his thought and action. Lincoln's words have remained eloquent through the generations because they reflect the profoundest truths of human experience. His writings bring inspiration to a democratic people because they are the expressions of a character unique in its humaneness and an intelligence remarkable in its understanding. Lincoln's essential greatness lay in the recesses of his mind and being, not in his techniques of group manipulation.

There was little in Lincoln's early life to separate him from his fellow men. Neither as a backwoods lawyer nor as an Illinois politician had he brought any measurable distinction on himself. Yet there was always a unique element in Lincoln's nature. As early as 1838 in a speech before the Young Men's Lyceum in Springfield, Illinois, he revealed that profound understanding of human action that characterized his later success. Lincoln first attained national prominence in the Lincoln-Douglas debates. His political adroitness in pinning down his opponent to an embarrassing position on popular sovereignty elevated him to a position of command in the Republican Party. Thereafter it was his management of the issues and the compromises on slavery that held the party together and molded it into a victorious organization by 1860. But if Lincoln's campaigning had unveiled his amazing grasp of the great questions confronting the nation, his election to the White House predicted neither greatness nor immortality.

Had Lincoln not been elected to the presidency during a crisis he might have remained obscure. Yet in office his moral dignity, his intellectual discipline, and his identification with great issues and events made him the instrument by which the Union would be preserved. This might have been accomplished without his assistance, but, Herbert Croly has observed, "the life of no other American has revealed with anything like the same completeness the peculiar moral promise of genuine democracy. He shows us by the full but unconscious integrity of his example the kind of human excellence which a political and social democracy may and should fashion; and its most grateful and hopeful aspect is, not merely that there is something partially American about the manner of his excellence, but that it can be fairly compared with the classic types of consummate personal distinction."

It would be presumptuous for the citizens of Illinois to lay some special claim to the man Lincoln. If his contribution to history did not transcend both time and place it would not merit the attention of an aspiring world. But even great men take some strength from their environment. Whatever his preparation for leadership before he entered the White House, it was a preparation wrought from the prairies of Illinois. If Lincoln belongs to the ages, this state can take some special pride in his achievements and some special sense of obligation from his example.

This small volume of lectures attempts to segregate from the vast Lincoln record those facets of his career which offer a perennial hope and an inescapable challenge to a troubled world. Specifically, these essays analyze his contribution to the democratic faith, to the principles of functioning democracy, to the management of the presidential office, and to the effective use of power and diplomacy in time of war. Lastly, this volume includes excerpts from the writings of Lincoln and Lincoln scholars which were on display in the University of Illinois Library during February, 1959. The common theme for these lectures, delivered on the Urbana-Champaign campus of the University of Illinois on February 11-12, 1959, is expressed in the title of the book.

To those who, as visiting lecturers, participated in this celebration so willingly the Sesquicentennial Committee is most grateful. It extends its appreciation as well to Gordon N. Ray, Vice President and Provost of the University of Illinois, for placing at the committee's disposal the necessary University resources.

Urbana   NORMAN A. GRAEBNER
February 12, 1959

THE ABRAHAM LINCOLN SESQUICENTENNIAL COMMITTEE

D. Alexander Brown · *Leslie W. Dunlap* · *Donald D. Jackson*
Donald W. Riddle · *Norman A. Graebner (Chairman)*

CONTENTS

ROY P. BASLER

Abraham Lincoln:
AN IMMORTAL SIGN

One approaches any anniversary with a sense of mystery and of ritual, for every anniversary is a reminder that something which began long ago is yet unfinished. And the questions of portent and meaning which confronted our fathers, and their fathers before them, remain with us, if not identical, still recognizable variations on a theme which neither they nor we have fully comprehended. So, on the sesquicentennial of Abraham Lincoln's birth one recognizes that repetition cannot be avoided, and seeks to make a virtue of necessity, citing Lincoln's own practice for justification. As a public speaker, Lincoln was one of the greatest repeaters in history, stating again and again some simple truths that needed repeating because, somehow, people were in his day, as in ours, great forgetters, who although they had often heard the truth, were unable to hold it fast much longer than an eighth grader can remember the lines he has memorized for a graduation exercise. We remember,

Roy P. Basler is director of the Reference Department, Library of Congress.

1

or should remember, in this age of conflict so similar in some respects to the age in which Lincoln lived, the memorable words of Lincoln, not because they bring ready-made answers to our problems, but because they may help us find our own answers and perhaps may even help us to phrase them.

I

It is a real temptation to do nothing on such an occasion but quote Lincoln, and perhaps one could do worse than merely read, with critical appreciation, the sculptured logic of his argument, savoring the poetic imagery and rhythms of his style. But, while not neglecting Lincoln's own words, perhaps it would be better, if one could do it, to try to formulate in brief the image of Lincoln which has become one of the enduring symbols in human history. Hence, what follows is an attempt to outline the major contribution which Lincoln made, not merely to the realm of thought and letters, but in a broad scope to human life itself, as a man once flesh and blood and brain, but long since become a symbol and a myth, a story in the annals of humanity which runs as an unfailing spring for whoever thirsts for truth.

I must ask indulgence, at this point, for a personal note, because I do not see how I can proceed without admitting that I am to some extent retracing my own steps in the study of Lincoln, and reaffirming some of the convictions which this study has established. More than twenty-five years ago I concluded the writing of a doctoral dissertation on the subject "Lincoln in Literature" (published in 1935 as a book entitled *The Lincoln*

Legend) with a quotation from Emerson's "Essay on History," which at that time seemed to me to summarize the forces which I thought I had identified at work in the many accounts of Lincoln's life — in biographical and historical writing no less than in the folklore, fiction, poetry, and drama with which I was chiefly concerned. Emerson had said the ultimate understanding of history demands that the student

attain and maintain that lofty sight where facts yield their secret sense, and poetry and annals are alike. The instinct of the mind, the purpose of nature, betrays itself in the use we make of the signal narrations of history. Time dissipates to shining ether the solid angularity of facts. No anchor, no cable, no fences, avail to keep a fact a fact. Babylon, Troy, Tyre, Palestine, and even early Rome are passing already into fiction. The Garden of Eden, the sun standing still in Gibeon, is poetry thenceforward to all nations. Who cares what the fact was, when we have made a constellation of it to hang in heaven an immortal sign?

At the sesquicentennial of Lincoln's birth, Emerson's philosophical and poetic comment furnishes not a conclusion but rather a point of departure for certain observations about the place which America's most representative historical figure has achieved in the story of mankind. The American people and the people of the world at large have adopted Lincoln as a symbol and have placed him as a star of the first magnitude in the firmament of historical heroes. Not a few writers, as well as artists in other media, have produced major works of art inspired by and assisting in the perpetuation of the symbolic myth of Lincoln. What is this symbol and what does it imply as one traces it in Lincoln literature?

It is in broadest terms the myth of a folk hero, noble in intellect, morally inspired, and imaginatively gifted, whose success was thwarted by the tragic flaw of ambiguity in the human nature which was his and his people's heritage. The myth itself is ambiguous, shifting and changing in its meaning as perceived and treated by different minds, but always revolving around the poles of a human nature that is dually free and constrained, right and wrong, good and bad. This mystery has been phrased and rephrased in every age and all languages, but nowhere more succinctly than by the Psalmist's question addressed to the Divine Being: "What is man that thou art mindful of him?" The gamut of human dilemmas in a moral universe is unrolled throughout the life and personality of Lincoln, in the broadly ambiguous terms which may be similarly traced in the more or less legendary heroes of the deep past from Adam to Arthur or from Caesar to Cromwell. And a primary lesson of history may be learned from the extent of a multitude of facts which do nothing to diminish, but rather enforce, the symbolic import, as read in the factual record, of the hero whose life has been more rather than less rigorously recorded and studied.

Thus the figure of Lincoln represents the American people. The questions, who was Lincoln, how did he happen, where was he going, what did he mean, why was he so, was he good or bad, did he achieve or fail — these are the questions we ask of ourselves. Who are we, how did we happen, where are we going, what do we mean, why are we so, are we good or bad, will we achieve or fail? The truth about Americans is the consistency of our contradictions, a practical and materialistic people but given to mysticism beyond measure, a selfish people whose largess has been demonstrated to surpass the richest myths of antiquity, a self-reliant people who are so filled with self-doubt that we crave more than anything else to be understood and appreciated — like a youth who believes in himself but wonders if after all he may not be a failure — an honest people who are shocked to discover our self-deceit and who strive to redefine our honesty to prevent self-deception. In Lincoln we have an epitome of what we are, we like to think, at our highest and best, as well as at our most ambiguous, and we would believe that the world could know us better by studying his life and works.

All of this may sound mystical, and it is. In an individual human being or in a society, it is the mystical, artistic, creative intelligence which seeks to make something more than a sequence of facts out of the experience of human life. Even when this search goes by the name of "seeking to understand," the dual process is in truth "making it thus," and philosophically "knowing" and "creating" become one. It is for this reason that the study of biography and history is ultimately much the same study as the study of poetry and fiction, and to some people perhaps, the more fascinating of the two disciplines. To know the truth of history is to realize its ultimate myth and its inevitable ambiguity.

If the development of this theme appears to be following a line of thought which has been overworked somewhat in recent years by a school of literary criticism, it may be noted that most new ideas are old ones in new dress, and that both Emerson and Lincoln developed

their similar philosophies of history before "symbolism,"
"myth," and "ambiguity" had become the shibboleths
of twentieth century academic criticism, but long after
Plato and Socrates had pondered many of the same
problems. In any case, the validity of this interpretation
must stand on its own feet, albeit indebted to many
thinkers besides Emerson, and including Lincoln, who
have recognized that factual reality may be, after all, but
a symbolic representation of a mystery, the meaning of
which remains yet to be solved.

II

To illustrate, let us consider two key incidents, each
with its set of circumstances amply if incompletely documented (there never has been complete documentation,
of course, for any historical event). The first is the so-
called beginning of the Civil War at Fort Sumter, and
the second is the emancipation of the slaves. These are
only two of many key incidents in the history of the
Civil War and in the public life of President Lincoln
which illustrate the ambiguity of the historical myth, but
they are chosen because they are well known and may
thus represent the problem better than several hundred
less known or even minor incidents in Lincoln's life
which could equally well illustrate the theme.

The question of who started the Civil War has obviously not been settled to date, as anyone who is willing
to read more than one book can demonstrate to his own
satisfaction. Even though the preponderant number of
opinions, if one counts opinions, or the preponderant
weight of opinion, if one weighs opinion, may seem to
indicate that the South started it by firing on Fort

Sumter, rather than that the North started it by "invading" Charleston Harbor with armed ships. When this question comes down to individuals, it is whether Lincoln started the war by ordering the expedition to relieve Fort Sumter, or whether any one of several assorted Confederates, ranging from General Beauregard, who certainly must have authorized the notification of intention to fire "within one hour" which bears the signatures of his Aides-de-Camp Chesnut and Lee, to Edmund Ruffin who is recorded as having fired the first gun. It is tragically humorous to reflect on the symbolic dispersal of even a "perhaps" assignment of final responsibility on the Confederate side. Every participant was *somewhat* responsible, but no individual was *finally* responsible in the Confederacy, least of all President Jefferson Davis, who was after all the President of a mere Confederacy. But on the Union side the symbolism is precisely the opposite; Lincoln was the final human authority, and he never questioned the fact himself, although he understood clearly that this was a symbolic authority vested in him by the ballots of the American people. He made it clear, even though he did not expect agreement from the Confederates, that his intention to hold Sumter (as a symbol, be it noted, for its value as a base of operations was neglible) was not regarded by him as an act of aggression. The penultimate paragraph of his First Inaugural Address stated the position from which he could not retreat.

In *your* hands, my dissatisfied fellow countrymen, and not in *mine,* is the momentous issue of civil war. The government will not assail *you.* You can have no conflict, without being yourselves the aggressors. *You* have no oath registered in Heaven to destroy the government, while *I* shall have the most solemn one to "preserve, protect and defend" it.

In his annual message to Congress, December 6, 1864, he reiterated in his final paragraph what he had said three and a half years earlier:

In stating a single condition of peace, I mean simply to say that the war will cease on the part of the government, whenever it shall have ceased on the part of those who began it.

Thus the mystery of who started the Civil War centers in the mind of Lincoln. Did he order the expedition to relieve Fort Sumter as a cunning trick to solicit the first blow from the Confederacy in order to pretend that he was attacked when in fact he was attacking? This is the implicit premise of many and the affirmed premise of some members of a school of thought which remains active, though in a minority, today. A more charitable as well as more philosophical way of putting the question would be: Did Lincoln order the expedition to relieve Fort Sumter as a symbolic force to illustrate to the secessionists that he did not recognize a symbolic sovereignty which most of the citizens of those states claimed to reside in fact in the state as opposed to the nation under the Constitution? There is this difference in the two questions. The first implies moral obliquity on the part of Lincoln, just as a similar obverse would imply moral obliquity on the part of Jefferson Davis and other secessionists; that is, did secessionists sponsor state sovereignty and the act of secession as a cunning trick in the guise of a moral right in order to perpetuate a ruling slavocracy in the South when it could no longer extend its power in the whole Union? The second question — did Lincoln order the expedition as a symbolic force to illustrate the symbolic sovereignty of the Union which he refused to abandon or to admit that the secessionists could abandon — not only implies but recognizes the political ambiguity of the Constitution itself on the matter of state versus federal sovereignty, as being the ultimate ambiguity which Lincoln hoped, if possible, to try to diminish gradually, if not to resolve finally, by ballots rather than bullets.

The whole question of who started the Civil War is thus a symbolic rather than a merely factual question, and it runs back, politically, psychologically, morally, and philosophically, to Cain and Abel and their distraughtly responsible father and mother. Who shall rule whom? Only the self-righteous, it seems to me, can read in Lincoln's Second Inaugural Address a statement of hypocrisy rather than a confession of sin and a prayer for absolution.

Both parties deprecated war; but one of them would *make* war rather than let the nation survive; and the other would *accept* war rather than let it perish. . . . Both read the same Bible, and pray to the same God; and each invokes His aid against the other. . . . The Almighty has his own purposes. "Woe unto the world because of offences! for it must needs be that offences come; but woe to that man by whom the offence cometh!" . . . Fondly do we hope — fervently do we pray — that this mighty scourge of war may speedily pass away. . . .

Where is the tragic ambiguity of the human condition more poignantly set forth than in the record of the Civil

War, where more poetically symbolized than in Lincoln, the hero who recognized this ambiguity in himself and in the people whom he represented, or where more memorably expressed than in his words?

III

The second incident chosen to illustrate the symbolic ambiguity of the Lincoln myth is the promulgation of the Emancipation Proclamation. Did Lincoln free the slaves? At the time, his antagonists were quick to attack the Proclamation as a hoax, because its language limited emancipation specifically to those areas which were under Confederate control, and hence where Lincoln had no operational authority. Here again we are confronted with a symbolic action, as ambiguous in its meaning as is the language of the Proclamation itself, and yet it is the turning point in Lincoln's presidency. In promulgating the Proclamation Lincoln burned a bridge behind him. Until September 22, 1862, the date on which the preliminary proclamation was issued stipulating January 1, 1863, as the date on which emancipation would take effect, Lincoln had not advanced much beyond the position he had stated in collaboration with his colleague in the Illinois legislature, Dan Stone, in a set of Resolutions entered in the *Illinois House Journal* under date of March 3, 1837, namely, "that the institution of slavery is founded on both injustice and bad policy . . . but that the Congress of the United States has no power, under the Constitution, to interfere with the institution of slavery in the different States." As late as August 22, 1862, he had written Horace Greeley, "If I could save the Union without freeing *any* slave, I would do it; and if I could save it by freeing *all* the slaves, I would do it; and if I could save it by freeing some and leaving others alone I would also do that." One month later he issued the preliminary proclamation which pledged:

That on the first day of January in the year of our Lord, one thousand eight hundred and sixty-three, all persons held as slaves within any state, or designated part of a state, the people whereof shall then be in rebellion against the United States shall be then, thenceforward, and forever free; and the executive government of the United States, including the military and naval authority thereof, will recognize and maintain the freedom of such persons, and will do no act or acts to repress such persons, or any of them, in any efforts they may make for their actual freedom.

This was a promise, the fulfillment of which required not only the winning of the war but also the later enactment of the Thirteenth Amendment and the Fourteenth Amendment, and yet it marked a turning point not only in American history but also in Lincoln's personal thinking about slavery — that armed force should be used to set the Negro free in the rebel states as a means to the end of saving the Union.

Thus a symbolic act and a purely symbolic document established whatever facts of freedom the Negro may enjoy in the South today, but if anyone supposes that the ambiguities of that act and that document have been finally clarified by any amendment to the Constitution, or by any court decision rendered to date, or by any executive action by the President of the present United States, he surely cannot have been reading the newspapers.

There have been no statues erected to Abraham Lincoln in the South, but if one were to be erected in recognition of this sesquicentennial it might well bear inscribed on its pedestal the passage which occurs in the second paragraph of Lincoln's opening speech in the fourth debate with Stephen A. Douglas at Charleston, Illinois, September 18, 1858. Segregationist literature has cited this passage so often that it is probably better known in the South today than anything else Lincoln wrote, including the Gettysburg Address. This is what Lincoln said:

I will say then that I am not, nor ever have been in favor of bringing about in any way the social and political equality of the white and black races, [applause] — that I am not nor ever have been in favor of making voters or jurors of negroes, nor of qualifying them to hold office, nor to intermarry with white people; and I will say in addition to this that there is a physical difference between the white and black races which I believe will for ever forbid the two races living together on terms of social and political equality. And inasmuch as they cannot so live, while they do remain together there must be the position of superior and inferior, and I as much as any other man am in favor of having the superior position assigned to the white race.

Of course, it would be expecting too much for the segregationists to quote the letter Lincoln wrote to Governor Michael Hahn of Louisiana on March 13, 1864, which indicates that Lincoln modified his views expressed at Charleston to some extent before he died. He wrote to Hahn as follows:

I congratulate you on having fixed your name in history as the first-free-state Governor of Louisiana. Now you are about to have a Convention which, among other things, will probably define the elective franchise. I barely suggest for your private consideration, whether some of the colored people may not be let in — as, for instance, the very intelligent, and especially those who have fought gallantly in our ranks. They would probably help, in some trying time to come, to keep the jewel of liberty within the family of freedom. But this is only a suggestion, not to the public, but to you alone.

Basically, we have in Lincoln's own words the unresolved ambiguity of freedom for the Negro. Is freedom the same for black as for white? Are all men created equal?

IV

All his political life Lincoln had been saying that the soul of America's being was the proposition that "all men are created equal." He had referred to this phrase in the Declaration of Independence many times during the campaign of 1858 in language which seems to be directly contradictory to the spirit and meaning of the language he used at Charleston; such as, for example, when he spoke at Chicago on July 10, calling it "the electric cord . . . that links the hearts of patriotic and liberty-loving men together, that will link those patriotic hearts as long as the love of freedom exists in the minds of men throughout the world." How, if at all, can we reconcile this apparent contradiction?

The Gettysburg Address is Lincoln's highest expression, in poetic, symbolic terms, of how he conceived of the Declaration of Independence, not as a statement of fact but as a symbolic proposition to the ultimate proving of which the nation was dedicated at its birth. Lincoln believed that "all men are created equal" in the only way that a mind as coldly logical as his could believe in it. Just how he believed it, is indicated by his use of the word "proposition." This word has proved a stumbling block even for highly literate readers who cannot conceive of the essential kinship of poetry and mathematics as creations of the human mind in the search for truth, and of both poetry and mathematics as theory providing a symbolic frame in which life may be understood. By his own account Lincoln had "studied and nearly mastered Euclid," and we may be sure that he used the word "proposition" naturally in the Euclidean sense of a statement to be debated, and if possible, verified or proved. Thus American democracy, as an active, living thing, meant to Lincoln the verification or proving of the proposition to which its very existence was in the beginning dedicated. In 1863, eighty-seven years had gone into the proving, the Civil War had come at a critical stage in the argument, the Union armies had won an inconclusive victory, and the affirmation that "all men are created equal" was still a live proposition, open to argument and inviting proof, but not on any account one that had already been proved. The further proof was for "us the living, to be dedicated here to the unfinished work which they who fought here have thus far so nobly advanced."

It was thus that Lincoln believed in democracy, not as an already proven principle, nor as a meaningless form of words incapable of proof, but as the most viable political proposition about human life which the human mind had been able to conceive in the long history of civilization. The Gettysburg Address suggests that Lincoln's understanding of history was not far from Emerson's: "Who cares what the fact was, when we have made a constellation of it to hang in heaven an immortal sign?"

Into Lincoln's concept was distilled the best thought of two thousand years of European civilization, striving to break the hold of tribal myth, to divest humanity of outworn social and political forms, and to create a political-social pattern in which men might live together without being either ruler or subject, master or slave. The concept was humanistic in that it projected the humanist's conviction that the mind of the individual man could give order and meaning to the impulse of the individual human life. To understand was to be free to act in harmony with fate in the pursuit of happiness. So Lincoln conceived the nation as a being with conflicting drives, hopes, and fears, but guided by reason — not all-knowing, but capable of learning and growing, and capable of regeneration in the midst of decay. For this nation, conceived in liberty and perpetuating the free spirit which gave it birth, could not die so long as men lived who gave of their life, their liberty, and their happiness to preserve it.

Hence Lincoln phrased one of the most memorable passages in the English language, as a symbolic statement of the meaning of facts long since laid to rest in the tomb of history, but resurrected in the bloody travail of civil war to live again in a new era:

Four score and seven years ago our fathers brought forth on this continent, a new nation, conceived in Liberty, and dedicated to the proposition that all men are created equal.

Now we are engaged in a great civil war, testing whether that nation, or any nation so conceived and so dedicated, can long endure. We are met on a great battle-field of that war. We have come to dedicate a portion of that field, as a final resting place for those who here gave their lives that that nation might live. It is altogether fitting and proper that we should do this.

But, in a larger sense, we can not dedicate — we can not consecrate — we can not hallow — this ground. The brave men, living and dead, who struggled here, have consecrated it, far above our poor power to add or detract. The world will little note, nor long remember what we say here, but it can never forget what they did here. It is for us the living, rather, to be dedicated here to the unfinished work which they who fought here have thus far so nobly advanced. It is rather for us to be here dedicated to the great task remaining before us — that from these honored dead we take increased devotion to that cause for which they gave the last full measure of devotion — that we here highly resolve that these dead shall not have died in vain — that this nation, under God, shall have a new birth of freedom — and that government of the people, by the people, for the people, shall not perish from the earth.

This symbolic conception of the Declaration of Independence was not new with Lincoln at Gettysburg, for he had many times before stated his recognition of the "immortal sign." One of his most pointed statements occurs in his letter to H. L. Pierce, April 6, 1859, written to be read at a festival honoring the birthday of Thomas Jefferson.

All honor to Jefferson — to the man who, in the concrete pressure of a struggle for national independence by a single people, had the coolness, forecast, and capacity to introduce into a merely revolutionary document, an abstract truth, applicable to all men and all times, and so to embalm it there, that to-day, and in all coming days, it shall be a rebuke and a stumbling-block to the very harbingers of re-appearing tyranny and oppression.

But Lincoln was fully aware of the ambiguity of equality and freedom for all men, and of the symbolic role of the Constitution as "the picture of silver" framing "the apple of gold." Freedom and equality are completely ambiguous except under symbolic authority, and the symbolism of the Constitution undertakes to resolve this complete ambiguity by breaking it down into many symbolic parts, each of which contains it own ambiguity, and all of which are collectively referred to, somewhat euphemistically, as "a system of checks and balances."

Who shall rule whom? As there is no absolute answer possible except an ambiguous one, so there can be no practical, wholly unambiguous answer in any specific case. Lincoln pointed out in his First Inaugural Address that "No organic law can ever be framed with a provision specifically applicable to every question which may occur in practical administration." And in differences of opinion (based on ambiguities) arises the necessity that someone must acquiesce. "If the minority will not acquiesce," Lincoln continued, "the majority must, or the government must cease. There is no other alternative; for continuing the government, is acquiescence on one side or the other." But acquiescence on one side or the other, under constitutional government, cannot resolve finally the ambiguity of the human condition in which "all men are created equal" and "are endowed by their Creator with certain unalienable rights." When Lincoln said on February 22, 1861, at Independence Hall, Philadelphia, that he would almost rather be assassinated than to give up that principle, he not only voiced recognition of the extreme to which a minority of one might go, but also avowed, in the strongest language he ever used, his own dedication to the most precious of all ambiguities, precious because, as he said, it gave hope "not alone to the people of this country, but, I hope, to the world, for all future time." Not in certainty but in ambiguity lay the hope which to Lincoln, as one man, gave scope and meaning to the individual's quest for identity. This is the ultimate truth of the myth of Lincoln which inspires the poetry, the fiction, the drama, the statues, and the factual biographies as well, and it is the ultimate truth likewise of the myth of the American nation whose people Lincoln represented and still represents.

V

So far we have dealt with the Lincoln myth in terms of the ambiguity of its meaning to those who have studied it, and who by trying to understand, have to some extent created its symbolic proportions as lasting truth. All this is preface to what remains to be said about Lincoln the artist—the creative spirit that molded out of the circumstances of daily life and the historical events of the era in which he lived, a personal myth for himself, which is remarkably like the myth that literature (including biography and history) has made of him. Lincoln's personal myth was the seed from which the historical myth has grown.

Lincoln's life was to him a quest for identity and a creation of identity, sparked by ambition so intense that no immediate failure could put it off and no success could satisfy its craving. This creative impulse, as with all men in some degree perhaps, took various channels, but two main currents — the political and the literary — run throughout his life and frequently blend into one. Lincoln seems never to have begun and never to have ceased to love to play with people and to play with words. This instinct was born with him. There is little reason to question the folk stories about his childhood oratory and versifying, or early proclivities for making friends and influencing people, when such activity produced the documented record of his maturity. The essential effort of his life was to identify himself, by words and in relationships to his contemporaries, as a representative, symbolic hero. He sought to play a role the action and words of which he would create for himself as circumstance and opportunity arose, but always with his mind's eye on the ultimate scene of the ultimate act, in which he would achieve his symbolic identity.

His first political address, dated March 9, 1832, announcing his candidacy for representative in the Illinois legislature, concluded with a candid statement of this mission:

Every man is said to have his peculiar ambition. Whether it be true or not, I can say for one that I have no other so great as that of being truly esteemed of my fellow men, by rendering myself worthy of their esteem. How far I shall succeed in gratifying this ambition, is yet to be developed.

After a quarter of a century, Lincoln's concept of his role had not materially changed. He had no pat solution to the problem of slavery, he sought to lead no crusade, but he hoped that in time the terrible ambiguity of human freedom and equality would gradually, in increasing measure, be resolved of necessity by new laws expressing the will of the majority, not of one state or one section, but of the United States. As to slavery, at that time the most that Lincoln hoped for, as he expressed it in the famous House Divided speech on June 16, 1858, was that "the public mind shall rest in the belief that it is in the course of ultimate extinction." By the end of the campaign, however, Lincoln had recognized slavery as the Nemesis of the personal role as hero which he had dreamed for himself. He concluded his last speech in the campaign on October 30, 1858, as follows:

Ambition has been ascribed to me. God knows how sincerely I prayed from the first that this field of ambition might not be opened. I claim no insensibility to political honors; but today could the Missouri restriction be restored, and the whole slavery question replaced on the old ground of "toleration" by *necessity* where it exists, with unyielding hostility to the spread of it, on principle, I would, in consideration, gladly agree, that Judge Douglas should never be *out,* and I never *in,* an office, so long as we both or either, live.

But this could not be, because Lincoln refused to accept as his final identity the role of a defeated Illinois politician, and because his Nemesis remained, still capable of dealing him, before the final retribution, an ambiguous success as President of a disintegrating nation. The ambiguity of his success was ever present to Lincoln's mind from the moment of his election onward. Of his many frank recognitions of this ambiguity none is more succinct than the statement in a letter he wrote on April 4, 1864, to A. G. Hodges, editor of the Frankfort (Kentucky) *Commonwealth.* "I claim not to have controlled events," Lincoln wrote, "but confess plainly that events have controlled me." This was his clear judgment of his role as President after three years of war.

Four months later, having achieved the major part of his heroic identity, he spoke in one of his briefest and best speeches to the 166th Ohio Regiment on August 22, 1864, as follows:

I beg you to remember this, not merely for my sake, but for yours. I happen temporarily to occupy this big White House. I am a living witness that any one of your children may look to come here as my father's child has. It is in order that each one of you may have through this free government which we have enjoyed, an open field and a fair chance for your industry, enterprise and intelligence; that you may all have equal privileges in the race of life, with all its desirable human aspirations.

Such is the myth, from log cabin to White House, and lacking only the tragic denouement which Lincoln was further to live and create for himself down to the last scene in Ford's Theater on a Good Friday night, to a large extent made probable, if not indeed inevitable, by every choice of action which led up to it — such is the myth which Lincoln created, in his quest for identity, out of the ambiguity of his human nature. It is his story, it is our story, it is the world's story. And what does it mean? Let us begin again to see if we can discover its meaning.

In a log cabin, on Knob Creek, in La Rue County, Kentucky, on February 12, 1809 . . .

But time has indeed "dissipated to shining ether the solid angularity" of that cabin, and its meaning is purely symbolic, "a constellation to hang in heaven an immortal sign." We must begin elsewhere. Anywhere will do.

Abraham Lincoln:
PRAGMATIC DEMOCRAT

When President Lincoln in May of 1862 revoked General Hunter's order freeing slaves in his department, Wendell Phillips exploded with frustrated wrath. "The President is a very slow man; an honest man, but a slow moving machine," cried the Boston abolitionist. "I think if we can nudge him a little, it will be of great advantage." But as the war continued, Phillips came to despair that the man in the White House could be nudged — fast enough or far enough. "Mr. Lincoln is not a leader," Phillips lamented. "His theory of Democracy is that he is the servant of the people, not the leader. . . . We pay dear today for having as President a man so cautious as to be timid. . . . As long as you keep the present turtle at the head of affairs, you make a pit with one hand and fill it with the other. I know Mr. Lincoln. . . . He is a mere convenience and is waiting like any other broomstick to be used." Most abolitionists subscribed to Phillips' evaluation of Lincoln, and they

T. Harry Williams is a professor of history at Louisiana State University.

retained their opinion even after the President threw his
support behind emancipation. In 1865, near the end of
the war, L. Maria Child, reminiscing about the final
victory of the antislavery cause, observed, "I think we
have reason to thank God for Abraham Lincoln." Despite all his deficiencies, she concluded with that conde-
scension peculiar to intellectuals, he had been a man
"who was willing to grow."

I

There was more in the abolitionist attitude than
merely a feeling that Lincoln was a good but not particularly bright man who had to be guided along the
right path. To such abolitionists as Phillips and such
dedicated Radical Republican leaders as George W.
Julian, Abraham Lincoln was a politician without principle. These men can be accurately classified under a
term popular in modern thought as "ideologues." They
had a definite and detailed ideology or philosophy, and
they had a precise blueprint for social reform based on a
preconceived abstract theory. They were prepared to
put their design into effect without much regard for the
opinions of those who opposed them and without much
thought of the problems that abrupt change might create. In describing their methods and goals they used
such phrases as "remorseless and revolutionary violence."
Their motto was that of intellectual radicals in all ages:
Let there be justice even though the heavens crumble
down. To such men—grim, certain, doctrinaire—Abraham Lincoln seemed theoretically backward. So also
must Andrew Jackson have seemed to the professional
expositors of Jacksonian Democracy, Theodore Roosevelt

to the advanced pundits of Progressivism, and Franklin D. Roosevelt to the social welfare philosophers of the New Deal. None of the great American political leaders has been a systematic thinker or an advocate of change for the sake of theory.

Lincoln believed deeply in certain fundamental political principles, but he never assumed to elevate his beliefs into a doctrine. And his opinions or ideas bore little if any resemblance to what is called ideology today. Lincoln would be patiently amused at the attempts of moderns to classify his thinking into some neat niche under some convenient label. We are familiar with and tolerantly scornful of the efforts of politicians and special interests to annex him for their own ends. He has been claimed by Republicans and Democrats, by parties from the far right to the distant left. He has been put forward as the spokesman of unbridled individualism — and of unrestrained statism. But the ax-grinders have not been the only classifiers. The academic scholars, perhaps influenced more than any other group in contemporary society by the concept of ideology and always convinced that a man's ideas can be arranged in a logical pattern, have tried their hand at pinning tidy thought tags on Father Abraham. Characteristically, they have come up with contradictory conclusions.

Some historians, noting Lincoln's tributes to equality of opportunity and the virtues of hard work, and his obvious caution in the face of change, have depicted him as the personification of the economic conservative. Other writers, impressed by the same evidence but giving it an opposite twist, have decided that Lincoln knew little about the economic trends of his times, that he was, in fact, almost an economic simpleton and possibly a folksy front for the industrial capitalism then rising to power. But most historians, responding to the intellectual climate of our day and reflecting their own beliefs, have made Lincoln a liberal, which by their definition means a modern Democrat. Citing his statements that human rights were above property rights, and his friendly words for labor, they have presented him as an early New Dealer, as a pre-Fort Sumter Franklin D. Roosevelt.

All these attempts to categorize Lincoln's thinking fall wide of the mark. Indeed, it is doubtful if easy, explanatory labels can be affixed to any of the American political leaders. The nature of our political system is so complex that no facile polarism can be imposed upon it, especially when the polarism employs such terms as conservative and liberal drawn from European usage. Lincoln, like Jefferson, Jackson, and the two Roosevelts, was a pragmatist. In his approach to social problems he represented the best tradition of British and American politics. The spirit of American pragmatic reform, Frederick Lewis Allen has suggested, may be illustrated by comparing society or the nation to a machine. If something goes wrong with the machine, what should one do? The reactionary might say, "Don't fool with it, you will ruin it." The radical might say, "It's no good, get rid of it and find a new one." But the pragmatist would try to fix the machine up, to remove the defective part and add a new one. Translated into political language, his attitude would be to make a needed change at the right time. American pragmatism has stressed the necessity for continuous, co-operative experimental reform — but it has also insisted, above all, that while changes are being made the machine must be kept running. A proposed change may be moral or theoretically right, but it has also to be demonstrably sound in the light of past experience and present realities.

Lincoln's political beliefs, or what might be termed his inner opinions, were based firmly on principle. His public or outer opinions were always restrained by his strong pragmatic sense, by his fine feeling for what, given the fact of human limitations, was politically possible. One of the keys to his thinking is his statement that few things in this world were wholly good or wholly evil. Instinctively Lincoln distrusted doctrinaire thinkers like the abolitionists who claimed to know what was good and evil, and who were prepared to act upon their opinions. He distrusted the abolitionists because they were blueprint people, because they proposed to make a change based on theory, because they would force this change over all resistance and without regard for social consequences. Lincoln was as much opposed to slavery as the abolitionists. "If slavery is not wrong," he said, "nothing is wrong." But he did not consider that he had the right, even as President, to translate his opinion into action and impose it on others. "I am naturally anti-slavery," he said in 1864. "And yet I have never understood that the Presidency conferred upon me an unrestricted right to act officially upon this judgment and feeling."

By temperament Lincoln was tolerant, patient, non-censorious. By nature he was practical, moderate, gradual. Being what he was, he preferred to see changes come slowly and after due deliberation and with the consent of all affected groups. Almost instinctively Lincoln inclined to a middle-of-the-road position on issues. "Stand WITH anybody that stands RIGHT," he advised the Whigs in 1854. "Stand with him while he is right and PART with him when he goes wrong. Stand WITH the abolitionist in restoring the Missouri Compromise; and stand AGAINST him when he attempts to repeal the fugitive slave law. In the latter case you stand with the Southern disunionist. What of that? . . . In both cases you are right. In both cases you expose the dangerous extremes. In both cases you stand on middle ground and hold the ship level and steady." A man who thought like this was definitely not the kind of leader desired by ideologues like Phillips — a leader who was ready to do what God would do if God had possession of all the facts.

II

The historians of intellectual life have emphasized that four primary principles formed the basis of American political philosophy in the middle years of the nineteenth century when Lincoln was growing into mental maturity. Americans might quarrel about the application of these principles to specific current issues, but to an extraordinary degree they were accepted as common beliefs, so much so that some writers have referred to them as articles of the national faith. The four ideas may be conveniently summarized:

(1) A supernatural power, God or a Guiding Providence or nature, exercised a controlling influence over the affairs of men. God had created a divine or higher law for the guidance of humans, and men could appre-

hend this law and should seek to approximate their own statutes to it.

(2) Man was not just another creature on the planet, but a being with a higher nature; or, as some put it, he had within him a spark of the divine. He had a mind, and hence could reason, and he had a conscience, and hence could distinguish right from wrong. This being true, he could govern himself through democratic forms and could achieve, if not perfectibility, a high degree of political maturity and a fair measure of happiness.

(3) The best economic system was one based on private ownership of property and one in which most people were property owners. The right to acquire property was a natural right, and all men should strive to secure property. Under the workings of the system, some would get more than others but no great inequities would result as long as equal opportunity existed. And no class or group should enjoy special privileges that gave it an artificial advantage over others.

(4) The American Union was a unique and precious experiment in government. As the most successful example of popular government in a big country, the United States was the supreme demonstration of democracy and the hope of world democracy. It made men free in America, and eventually by the sheer force of its example would make them free everywhere. Americans were profoundly conscious of the Union's value to themselves and of its universal mission. This consciousness was one of the strongest forces sustaining American nationalism.

Lincoln took over all four of the common beliefs of his time and made them a part of his own thought. This is not to say that he borrowed them blindly or adopted them without analysis. Such a procedure would have been foreign to Lincoln's nature. Every idea he ever held was the result of long and tough thinking, of introspective brooding during which he turned a proposition over and over in his mind. When he finally arrived at the formulation of a fundamental principle, it usually became a permanent part of his mental make-up. Nevertheless, Lincoln must be classified as a derivative rather than a seminal thinker, as an expresser — in superb words — rather than an originator of ideas. He did, however, give a significant extension to one of the four principles, the exaltation of the American Union.

Statements attesting Lincoln's belief that a supernatural force controlled human activities are sprinkled throughout his public and private papers, and they appear in practically every phase of his political career. Even in his early years he was intrigued by the concept of this compelling force, which he sometimes called history. As he grew older he came to call it God. For most Americans, the notion of a Guiding Providence meant only that a benign deity exercised a general influence over the affairs of men and that within the divine framework men had some freedom to work out their destinies. History was not a haphazard process tending to nowhere in particular, but a progressive movement that was being guided toward a definite and high goal.

But Lincoln, with a deep mystic strain in his nature and with a constant sense of fatalism, both public and personal, pushed this idea farther than most. It is no exaggeration to say that during the Civil War he developed a mechanistic interpretation of history. The great event with which his name is associated, the destruction of slavery, was, he believed, an act of divine power of which he was but the instrument. In a remarkable letter written in 1864 he reviewed the course of wartime emancipation, and then he added, "I claim not to have controlled events, but confess plainly that events have controlled me." In 1861 nobody had "devised, or expected" that the war would end slavery but now the institution was approaching extinction. "God alone can claim it. Whither it is tending seems plain. If God now wills the removal of a great wrong, and wills also that we of the North as well as you of the South, should pay fairly for our complicity in that wrong, impartial history will find therein new cause to attest and revere the justice and goodness of God." Lincoln stressed this theme again in the Second Inaugural Address when he said that the war was God's way of removing the evil of slavery as a punishment to both the North and the South for having condoned it. He realized that his ascription of inexorability would offend some people. "Men are not flattered by being shown that there has been a difference between the Almighty and them," he told Thurlow Weed. "To deny it, however, in this case, is to deny that there is a God governing the world."

The corollary to the principle of a supernatural power, the existence of a supernatural law, also formed a part of Lincoln's thought, but in his application of the principle to current issues he parted company with some of his fellow workers in the antislavery movement. From a reading of his papers, it is obvious that Lincoln believed there was a moral or higher law. "I hold," he said in the First Inaugural Address, "that in contemplation of universal law, and of the Constitution, the Union of these States is perpetual." It is just as obvious that he thought the Constitution approximated the spirit of divine law and embodied the best experience of man in government. He saw, or as Carl Sandburg has said, he sensed, that in a democracy there must be a balance between freedom and responsibility. The great merit of the American federal system was that it provided a balance between the government and the individual and between the nation and the states. Lincoln addressed himself to one of the fundamental problems of political science when, with his own government in mind, he asked: "Must a government, of necessity, be too strong for the liberties of its own people, or too weak to maintain its own existence?" The American system of divided powers, he thought, provided the only answer: "A majority, held in restraint by constitutional checks, and limitations, and always changing easily, with deliberate changes of popular opinions and sentiments, is the only true sovereign of a free people. Whoever rejects it, does of necessity, fly to anarchy or to despotism."

Lincoln accepted the principle of a higher law, but he refused to give it the logical extension, logical in theory, that some opponents of slavery gave it. If the supernatural law was perfect, it followed that human statutes that contravened it were illegal and must be changed. And if they could not be changed, they should not be obeyed. Some of the antislavery people persuaded themselves that the divine law concept justified the violation of any law protecting slavery. This was what William H. Seward meant when, in hurling defiance at the Fugitive Slave Act, he said, "There is a higher law than the

Constitution." Lincoln also disliked the fugitive slave measure, but he could never have agreed to the idea that individuals could flout it, or any other law, merely because it conflicted with their interpretation of higher law. In some countries it might be necessary for men to defy the law, but in the United States, where change was easy and deliberate, such action was unnecessary and irresponsible. It constituted a flying to anarchy.

Lincoln's confidence in the competence of men to govern themselves, in the democratic experiment, is apparent in his every political act from the Illinois legislature to the White House. Nowhere in his writing is expressed any doubt of majority rule or any fear of the tyranny of numbers. "Why should there not be a patient confidence in the ultimate justice of the people?" he asked in the First Inaugural Address. "Is there any better, or equal hope, in the world?" At the same time it is evident that Lincoln did not accept completely the roseate diagnosis of human nature that was so popular in the nineteenth century. This principle of the democratic faith was taken by some to mean that man, good, intelligent, and possessing a higher nature, was capable of approaching perfectibility and of achieving a perfect society. Such an optimistic prognosis was too much for Lincoln to swallow; it ran counter to his observation of reality. We don't have to read the Bible to find out that men are bad, he is supposed to have said, we can tell that by looking around us.

Rather than believing in the perfectibility of man, Lincoln thought that man was imperfect but was, nevertheless, the best instrument with which to accomplish the divine purpose. Rejecting the dream of unlimited social progress, Lincoln still believed that man was capable of improving himself and of increasing his political competence. His analysis was closer to the practical ideas of the Founding Fathers than to the romantic ideals of the thinkers of his own time. Lincoln readily grasped that the Fathers had not tried to establish a system of government based on human perfectibility but instead had created one that would enable men to raise progressively the level of their political maturity. In one of those "Fragments" in which he was wont to record his thinking, Lincoln wrote: *"Most governments* have been based, practically, on the denial of equal rights of men . . . ; *ours* began, by *affirming* those rights. They said, some men are too *ignorant,* and *vicious,* to share in government. Possibly so, said we; and, by your system, you would always keep them ignorant and vicious. We proposed to give *all* a chance; and we expected the weak to grow stronger, the ignorant wiser; and all better, and happier together. . . ."

It is Lincoln's economic thought that has provoked the widest differences of opinion among students of his life. The confusion derives from an attempt to apply labels, liberal and conservative, that have little applicability to the American scene, at least to the nineteenth century, and to a tendency of authors to project their own ideas and their images of the economic institutions of their day backward into time. Actually, Lincoln's economic views cannot be called either liberal or conservative in our sense of the words. Economics-wise he belongs to no party or group today, certainly not to the Republican and positively not to the New Deal. His economic concepts were completely the product of the economic system that he knew, and that system bears little resemblance to our own.

Lincoln grew to maturity during the preindustrial age of America's history; he became President when the nation stood at the threshold of the era of big business. Industrial combinations in the form that developed in the years after Appomattox did not exist. It is true that there were substantial aggregations of capital, especially in the Northeast, but these organizations and their future economic implication did not impress Lincoln and most Americans. (The opinion of some writers that Lincoln had only a very general understanding of economic matters is probably correct.) In the system that Lincoln saw about him — and this was particularly true of his own section, the Northwest — a large number of people owned property, in the shape of farms, factories, and shops, and made their living from the operation of their holdings. Unlike the present system, relatively few people worked for other people for wages or salaries. Many owners of property were also laborers in the sense that they worked in their own establishments. In short, this was a capitalistic economy that contained a lot of capitalists.

Lincoln's economic ideas were those of the average small capitalist of his time. It might be said that Lincoln and most Americans were "men on the make." That is, they wanted to raise their material standing by exercising the virtue of acquisitiveness. They saw nothing wrong with the drive to acquire property; indeed, they tended to glorify the property-getting process as a social good. In Lincoln's opinion the great merit of the American economic system was that it offered an equal opportunity to all men to secure property. And in his view equal opportunity would result in a system in which most men owned property. Lincoln respected labor, and he attested his respect in notable words on a number of occasions. Thus in his annual message to Congress in December, 1861, he said: "Labor is prior to, and independent of, capital. Capital is only the fruit of labor, and could never have existed if labor had not first existed. Labor is the superior of capital, and deserves much the higher consideration." But Lincoln's tributes to labor are usually misunderstood and misapplied today. They were not delivered to labor as a rival power to capital but to labor as a means of creating capital. Through his labor a man could become an owner or an employer. Lincoln always vehemently denied that American society was divided into two rigid classes of employers and employees. Most men, he argued, neither worked for others nor hired others to work for them; rather, they worked for themselves and were both capitalists and laborers. "There is no permanent class of hired laborers amongst us . . . ," Lincoln contended. "The hired laborer of yesterday labors on his own account to-day; and will hire others to labor for him to-morrow. Advancement — improvement in condition — is the order of things in a society of equals."

No great inequalities would result from the free competition for property, Lincoln thought, as long as the opportunities to compete were equal to all. In a speech at New Haven in 1860 he gave perhaps the fullest expression of his economic views. "What is the true condition of the laborer?" he asked. "I take it that it is best for all to leave each man free to acquire property as fast

as he can. Some will get wealthy. I don't believe in a law
to prevent a man from getting rich; it would do more
harm than good. When one starts poor, as most do in
the race of life, free society is such that he knows he can
better his condition; he knows that there is no fixed
condition of labor, for his whole life." Lincoln's optimistic vision of economic progress may seem naïve to
later liberals, and it probably has only a limited validity
for the problems of our day. But for his time it was valid
enough. By much the same process that he described,
Lincoln himself had risen from laborer to capitalist.

III

Of the four principles comprising the current creed of
his time, the one that aroused Lincoln's deepest devotion
was the exaltation of the American Union. This idea, or
this image, of nationalism elicited the most frequent and
the most eloquent passages in his writings, and to it he
gave a significant extension that constitutes his only original contribution to political theory. It may be added
that as a political actor Lincoln's chief concern was with
nationality. When we say that as President he saved the
Union, we are also saying that he preserved the nation
— as both an abstraction and a physical reality. Perhaps Lincoln's truest title is not the Great Emancipator
but the Great Nationalist. Three ideas stand out in
Lincoln's concept of the nature and the significance of
the Union. They, too, may be conveniently presented in
itemized form:

(1) The nation was an organic whole, an entity that
could never be artificially separated by men. The realities of geography — rivers, mountains, ocean boundaries

— demanded that the United States remain united. Where, he asked the South in 1861, could a satisfactory line of division be drawn between two American nations? "Physically speaking, we cannot separate. We cannot remove our respective sections from each other, nor build an impassible wall between them." In his message to Congress in December, 1862, he gave a moving and also an exceedingly realistic description of the oneness of the United States, of what he called the "national home-stead." The outstanding American geographical fact, he emphasized, was the great interior heartland of the Mississippi Valley dominating the whole nation. Did anyone really believe, he asked, that the Mississippi River could be permanently divided by a man-made line? The present strife between the North and the South had not sprung from any natural division between the sections, he insisted, but from differences among people, "the passing generations of men." The land, the national homestead, "in all its adaptations and aptitudes . . . demands unity, and abhors separation. In fact, it would, ere long, force reunion, however much of blood and treasure the separation might have cost."

(2) The American nation was uniquely different from all others in the cementing bond that held it together. Some nations were united by race, some by culture, some by tradition. But the United States, said Lincoln in his most original piece of thinking, was bound by an idea, the principle of equal opportunity for all that was pledged in the Declaration of Independence and em-bedded in the national consciousness. In a speech at Independence Hall in Philadelphia while on his way to Washington in 1861 to be inaugurated President, Lin-

coln tried to express what he thought was America's
great idea. "I have often inquired of myself, what great
principle or idea it was that kept this Confederacy so
long together," he said. "It was not the mere matter of
separation from the motherland, but that sentiment in
the Declaration of Independence which gave liberty not
alone to the people of this country, but hope to the
world for all future time. It was that which gave promise that in due time the weights would be lifted from the
shoulders of all men, and that *all* should have an equal
chance."

(3) American nationality was not a narrow thing intended only for the benefit of Americans. The Union
and the idea it represented made men free in America
and sooner or later by the power of its example would
make them free everywhere. Lincoln was supremely
conscious of the world mission of his country. Always
during the Civil War he tried to lift the Northern cause
to a higher level than victory for one section or even the
nation. Always he attempted to show that the preservation of the Union was important for the universal family
of mankind. The war was "a people's content" to
maintain "in the world, that form and substance of
government, whose leading object" was "to elevate the
condition of men." The "great republic . . . the principles it lives by, and keeps alive" represented "man's
vast future." It was "the last, best hope of earth."

IV

The great problem that faced the men of Lincoln's
time was slavery. In his thinking about slavery Lincoln
applied to the problem all four of the principles that

formed the substance of his general political faith. He
was opposed to slavery on moral, democratic, and economic grounds. He thought that it was wrong for one
man to own another. He feared that the presence of
slavery in American society would subvert the idea of
equal opportunity. If the notion that Negroes did not
possess equal economic rights became fixed, he said,
then the next easy transition would be to deny the same
rights to white laborers. He believed that slavery gave a
tone of hypocrisy to the claim that the United States
symbolized the democratic cause and thus endangered
the success of America's world mission.

Yet in his approach to the problem of slavery, Lincoln
was completely pragmatic and practical. He outlined
his position as early as 1837 in resolutions which he and
a colleague presented in the Illinois legislature declaring
that slavery was founded on "injustice and bad policy"
but that Congress had no power to interfere with it in
the states where it existed. To Lincoln one fact in the
situation — a fact that the abolitionists and other sincere
antislavery people ignored — was of vital importance:
slavery existed in the United States and millions of people believed in it. The physical presence of slavery and
the feelings of its Southern supporters, he argued, had to
be taken into account by the opponents of the institution. "Because we think it wrong, we propose a course
of policy that shall deal with it as a wrong," he said.
But, he immediately added, "We have a due regard to
the actual presence of it amongst us and the difficulties
of getting rid of it in any satisfactory way and all the
constitutional obligations thrown about it."

Again differing with most antislavery men and show-

ing a keen awareness of social behavior, Lincoln refused
to criticize the Southern people for supporting slavery.
"They are just what we would be in their situation," he
said at Peoria in 1854. "If slavery did not now exist
amongst them, they would not introduce it. If it did now
exist amongst us, we should not instantly give it up." In
this Peoria speech Lincoln dealt with the racial problems
that would inevitably follow the destruction of slavery.
The question of racial adjustment was inextricably con-
nected with emancipation. If the Negroes were freed,
what would be their place in society? The abolitionists
favored, at least abstractly, a status of complete equality
for the colored people. But most antislavery men, particularly if they were politicians, which was usually the
case, hardly ever discussed the position of the Negroes
after freedom. They had not thought the problem
through, probably did not want to think it to a conclusion. Perhaps this was one of the tragedies of the antislavery movement.

Lincoln admitted at Peoria, as he did on other occasions, that he did not know any absolutely satisfactory
way of dealing with slavery and the related racial problem. If all earthly power were given him, he said, he
would not know what to do. His first impulse would be
to free the slaves and remove them outside the United
States, but he conceded that this "colonization" plan
was impractical and impossible. What of the proposal
to give the freed slaves an equal place in society? This
would not do, Lincoln thought, because the mass of
white people South *and* North would not agree to such a
status for colored people. And whether the feelings of the
whites were just was beside the point, he said, because

"A universal feeling, whether well or ill founded, cannot be safely disregarded." Lincoln's own feelings about race are not easily comprehended by modern men. Personally, he had no color prejudices, as his relations with Negroes while President amply attest. But like perhaps ninety-nine per cent of Americans in the nineteenth century, he believed that the colored race, either by nature or by cultural inheritance, was inferior to the white race. Under any system of racial relations and even if the Negroes were free, the superior whites would seek to oppress the lesser race. Immediate emancipation, Lincoln feared, would not therefore benefit either race and would create for the Negroes problems almost as troublesome as those of slavery. As Professor Donald has pointed out, Lincoln's views may not be palatable to the modern reformer but they were an accurate analysis of current American opinion.

Lincoln opposed slavery, but he also opposed the abolitionists — the ideologues who wanted to destroy it immediately and who were certain that they had an absolutely satisfactory way of solving race relations. He disliked their readiness to impose their inner opinions on others, their eagerness to enforce a great social change based on a moral theory. He distrusted their abstract approach to a complex situation and their refusal to admit that all kinds of practical problems would result from a sudden change in that situation. Above all, he was appalled by their willingness to give up the Union if they could not make it over in their image. To him the preservation of American nationality was infinitely more important than the accomplishment of immediate emancipation. "Much as I hate slavery," he said, "I would consent to the extension of it rather than to see the Union dissolved, just as I would consent to any great evil, to avoid a greater one."

At the same time that he attacked the abolitionists' solution, Lincoln put forward his own plan to deal with the problem of slavery. It was to prevent slavery from expanding into the national territories, to pen it up in the states where it already existed. His proposal, he liked to say, would place slavery where the public mind could rest in the assurance that it was in "the course of ultimate extinction." If slavery could not grow, he argued, it would eventually wither and die a natural death. During the interim years, as the institution declined in social health, plans could be worked out for its orderly demise. The slaveholders themselves, perceiving the inevitable, would consent to emancipation and would receive financial compensation from the national government for the loss of their property. This kind of patient abolition, Lincoln thought, would bring in its wake no unfortunate results for either whites or blacks. Lincoln's plan would have taken years to effect, possibly a generation or more, but, and this is often forgotten by some of its critics, it was intended as a fundamental settlement of a problem that had to be settled finally. Lincoln's whole position on the slavery issue was in the finest American pragmatic tradition. He opposed immediate abolition because it would make a right change at the wrong time, would wreck the machine of the Union. He proposed to keep the machine going and to make the change later when the time was right.

Lincoln's plan for a gradual solution of the slavery problem never had a chance. There were too many men in the North and the South who could not wait that long, who were determined to settle the issue immediately, even if they had to resort to force. And so the Civil War came, and Lincoln became the President of a divided Union. He became also the leader of a divided North, of a people who differed among themselves as to the objectives of the war they were fighting. Specifically the question in issue was whether emancipation should be made one of the war aims. The discord in Northern opinion was reflected in Lincoln's own Republican party in the struggle between the Radical and the Conservative factions. The Radicals wanted to use the opportunity of the war to strike down slavery; they demanded that the Union be restored without slavery. Lincoln and the Conservatives hoped to avoid turning the war into a crusade for social change; he and most Conservatives preferred to restore the Union with slavery still intact.

To Lincoln the preservation of the Union, of American nationality, was the great overriding object of the war. The Union dwarfed all other issues, including slavery. Lincoln intended to save the Union by whatever methods he had to use. As he told Horace Greeley, to accomplish his purpose he would, if necessary, free all of the slaves or free none of them or free some and keep others in bondage. At the same time he understood clearly the dynamics in the war situation. He knew that slavery was the provoking cause of the conflict. Slavery was "the disturbing element" in "the national house," he said, and it would continue to generate strife until it was removed. He knew, too, that the antislavery impulse would receive a tremendous impetus from the war. Lincoln approached slavery during the war in the same pragmatic spirit with which he had dealt with it before the war. He was ready to end it, as he would any other social evil, if he was convinced that the time was right and that greater evils would not result from its destruction.

At the beginning of hostilities Lincoln proposed that the sole objective of the war should be restoration of the Union. His immediate purpose was to bring all parties and factions in the North together in support of a war for the nation. This required a statement of war aims so simple and so national that all groups could unite behind it. But beyond the exigencies of public opinion, Lincoln did not want emancipation to become one of the war aims. He did not want slavery to be destroyed suddenly in the anger of civil conflict. If slavery was uprooted as a part of the war process, the change would be too violent; such a change would make it difficult, if not impossible, to solve the related problem of race relations. At the same time he realized that the situation created by the war demanded a more urgent approach to emancipation; a plan had to be worked out *now* to place slavery in the course of extinction. In an effort to provide such a plan, Lincoln, on several occasions, asked the border states congressmen to join with him in initiating a scheme for compensated gradual emancipation. With singular blindness they ignored his ideas.

Inevitably the facts of the war made Lincoln's hopes and plans for a gradual, orderly reform of the slavery problem impossible. Only in a short war, as he probably realized, could he have carried his policy. The longer the struggle continued, the more hostile Northern opinion became to slavery. It was unnatural that the Northern people would fight and sacrifice, for any period, to preserve an institution that in the opinion of most was the cause of the war. By the summer of 1862 every political sign indicated that the Northern masses wanted slavery destroyed as a result of the war. Now Lincoln faced a dilemma. If he opposed the popular will, if he persisted in postponing a settlement of the slavery issue to some future date, he would divide Northern opinion and perhaps wreck the entire war effort. He would, and this was the vital point, defeat his larger objective of preserving American nationality. If he wanted to keep the machine running, he had to make a change; if he did not, the machine might break down.

For Lincoln there could be only one response and one action. It was at this time that he decided to issue the Emancipation Proclamation and to make emancipation a second aim of the war. He changed his position because the impelling dynamics of war had created a new situation that demanded a new policy. To the theoretical moralist, to the intellectual reformer, to the prophet of blueprints, his shift may seem unprincipled and opportunistic. Actually, Lincoln's stand on slavery was always completely moral. Before the war he had opposed abolition because it would destroy the Union. During the war he used abolition to save the Union. He opposed a right change at the wrong time and supported the same change at the right time. His course is the supreme example in our history of the union of principle and pragmatism in politics.

DAVID DONALD

Abraham Lincoln:
WHIG IN THE WHITE HOUSE

The presidency of Abraham Lincoln poses a peculiar paradox to students of the American government. The most careful historian of the Civil War period, J. G. Randall, concluded that Lincoln extended the President's "sphere of activity throughout the whole government — civil and military, state and Federal, legislative and judicial as well as executive." A distinguished political scientist, W. E. Binkley, agrees that Lincoln unquestionably set "the high-water mark of the exercise of executive power in the United States." On the other hand, Edward S. Corwin, who has made a lifelong study of the American presidency, notes that Lincoln, "a spoilsman" with no conception of the requirements of sound administration, failed to exert much influence over Congress and permitted the Civil War to be fought "by a kind diarchy," with each end of Pennsylvania Avenue carrying on its own campaign against the Confederates. Recognizing that Lincoln "added a new dimension to the Presidency in the presence of national

David Donald is a professor of history at Columbia University.

emergency," Professor Corwin concludes that his incumbency was "in certain other respects a calamity for the office." The paradox has been most neatly posed in an able book, *The American Presidency,* by Clinton Rossiter, who asserts on one page that "Lincoln pushed the powers of the Presidency to a new plateau high above any conception of executive authority hitherto imagined in this country," but adds on the next that "Lincoln . . . left the Presidency temporarily enfeebled."

I

For the view that Lincoln dramatically extended the range of executive power there is certainly abundant evidence. In 1861 when the Confederates fired upon Fort Sumter he acted with such vigorous promptness that his critics cried out against his "dictatorship." Without consulting Congress, he decided that a state of war existed, summoned the militia to defeat this combination "too powerful to be suppressed by the ordinary course of judicial proceedings," and enlarged the size of the regular United States army. Without congressional appropriation or approval he entrusted two million dollars of government funds to his private agents in New York in order to pay for "military and naval measures necessary for the defense and support of the government." Directing General Winfield Scott "to suspend the writ of Habeas Corpus for the public safety," he authorized the arbitrary arrest of suspected secessionists and other enemies of the government.

As the war progressed Lincoln further extended his executive powers, even in the loyal states of the Union. "[B]y degrees," as he explained in 1863, he had come to feel that "strong measures" were "indispensable to the public Safety." Civil rights throughout the North were drastically curbed. Both Secretary of State William H. Seward, who was in charge of the arbitrary arrests made during 1861, and Secretary of War Edwin M. Stanton, who took control in the following year, exercised power "almost as free from restraint as a dictator or a sultan." Nobody knows how many Northern civilians were imprisoned without due process of law; estimates range from fifteen thousand to thirty-eight thousand. It required but a line from the President to close down a censorious newspaper, to banish a Democratic politician, or to arrest suspected members of a state legislature.

Over the Union armed forces, too, Lincoln exercised unprecedented authority. Presidential order, not congressional enactment, instituted in 1862 the first national program of conscription in United States history. Disregarding the explicit constitutional provision that Congress should "make Rules for the Government and Regulation of the land and naval Forces," Lincoln authorized Professor Francis Lieber to draw up and General Henry W. Halleck to proclaim General Orders No. 100, spelling out the legal rules for the conduct of the war.

Lincoln took quite literally the constitutional provision that "The President shall be Commander in Chief of the Army and Navy of the United States." He not merely appointed and removed generals; he attempted to plan their campaigns. At his insistence General Irvin McDowell advanced to First Bull Run and to defeat in July, 1861. Lincoln's unsolicited strategic advice drove General George B. McClellan, McDowell's successor, into hiding at the house of a friend so as to escape "browsing presidents." During the winter of 1861 when McClellan, ill with typhoid, did not advance, Lincoln issued his unprecedented President's General War Order No. 1, taking personal direction of five Union armies and two naval flotillas and ordering them simultaneously to advance on February 22. The fact that General McClellan, upon recovering, persuaded Lincoln to abandon his plan did not mean the end of presidential war-making. In fact, even at the end of the war, after Lincoln had named U. S. Grant general-in-chief, the President continued to have a personal hand in shaping Union strategy. Lincoln himself bluntly declared that should he think any plan of campaign ill-advised, he "would scarcely allow the attempt to be made, if the general in command should desire to make it."

To an even greater extent Lincoln asserted his presidential powers over the rebellious South. His Emancipation Proclamation, which Charles A. Beard called "the most stupendous act of sequestration in the history of Anglo-Saxon jurisprudence," was a presidential act, performed without authorization from Congress — performed, indeed, when the President thought Congress had no power to authorize it. Lincoln's December, 1863, proclamation of amnesty and pardon marked another major expansion of presidential powers. Without the approval of Congress he established provisional courts in conquered Southern states and gave them "the unlimited power of determining every question that could be the subject of judicial decision." In naming military governors for the states of Louisiana, Arkansas, and Tennessee, the President, again without congressional authorization, created offices unknown to the American Constitution. In establishing new and securely loyal administrations in these ex-Confederate states, the military governors were not obliged to observe normal constitutional procedures. Lincoln himself directed them: "Follow forms of law as far as convenient. . . ."

Lincoln's record, then, abundantly justifies the conclusion of George Fort Milton that no other President in American history has "found so many new sources of executive power, nor so expanded and perfected those others already had used."

II

But there is another aspect of the Lincoln administration. Less than any other major American President did Lincoln control or even influence the Congress. Noting that many of the Civil War congressmen were his seniors and humbly declaring "that many of you have more experience than I, in the conduct of public affairs," Lincoln bowed not merely to the will but to the caprice of the legislators. In making appointments, he regularly deferred to the Republican delegation from each state. He acquiesced in the Senate's right to veto appointments by refusing to resubmit any nomination which the Senate had rejected. Even upon a matter so clearly within presidential prerogative as extending recognition to Haiti and Liberia, Lincoln declined to act until Congress assented, because, he declared, he was

"Unwilling . . . to inaugurate a novel policy . . . without the approbation of Congress."

The President had remarkably little connection with the legislation passed during the Civil War. He proposed few specific laws to Congress; his bill for compensated emancipation is notably exceptional. He exerted little influence in securing the adoption of bills that were introduced. In some of the most significant legislation enacted during his administration Lincoln showed little interest. The laws providing for the construction of a Pacific railroad, for the creation of the Department of Agriculture, for the importation of "contract laborers" from Europe, for the tariff protection of American manufacturers, and for the establishment of land-grant colleges had little connection with Lincoln aside from his formal approval of them. That approval was usually granted without hesitation. Less than any other important American President did Lincoln use his veto power. He vetoed only two measures outright, an unimportant bill concerning bank notes in the District of Columbia and an act dealing with army medical officers which carelessly duplicated another he had already signed. One of his two pocket vetoes was equally trivial. The other, his highly significant refusal to sign the Wade-Davis Bill, indicated that the President thought that reconstruction was an executive, not a legislative, responsibility. Within the area of what he considered legitimate congressional power Lincoln was careful never to interfere.

Lincoln was also ineffectual in controlling the executive departments of the government. He and his cabinet never formed a unified administration. During his first

months as President, Lincoln did not schedu
cabinet meetings at all. When he later did
request of the cabinet members themselves,
discussed major policy decisions with his con
advisers. Sometimes the President himself was not
present at these meetings, and soon the department
heads became lax in attendance. The Secretary of State
preferred to meet with the President privately — to
regale him, enemies said, with vulgar stories; the Secretary of War declined to discuss his plans in cabinet
meeting because he thought, with some justice, that his
colleagues could not be trusted with military secrets;
Salmon P. Chase, the Secretary of the Treasury, refused
to waste his time attending sessions of this "so-called
Cabinet." "We . . . are called members of the Cabinet," Chase indignantly protested, "but are in reality
only separate heads of departments, meeting now and
then for talk on whatever happens to come uppermost,
not for grave consultation on matters concerning the
salvation of the country."

To most of his departmental chiefs Lincoln gave a
completely free hand. His Attorney-General, Postmaster-
General, Secretary of the Interior, and Secretary of the
Navy conducted their departmental affairs virtually
without oversight or interference from the President.
Even over a critical area like the Treasury Department
Lincoln exerted little control. Though some of the most
important financial legislation in American history was
adopted during the Civil War years, Lincoln had little
interest in floating bond issues, creating an internal
revenue system, inaugurating the first income tax, or
establishing a national banking system. Repeatedly

Chase tried to bring such weighty issues to the President's attention, but Lincoln brushed him aside, saying: "You understand these matters: I do not."

Even in the conduct of foreign relations the President himself played a minor role. It is a charming fancy to think of Lincoln as a "diplomat in carpet slippers," applying homely common sense and frontier wisdom to the preservation of international peace. In fact, however, after curbing Seward's belligerent tendencies early in 1861, the President willingly left diplomacy to his able Secretary of State. In Lincoln's *Collected Works* there is notably little about foreign affairs, aside from routine diplomatic communications, which were of course written by Seward, extending congratulations to Alexander II of Russia upon the birth of a son named "Pierre to Madame the Grand Duchess Alexandra Petrovna, Spouse of Your Imperial Majestys well beloved brother His Imperial Highness Monseigneur the Grand Duke Nicholas Nicolaewitch" or offering condolences upon the demise of "His Royal Hig[h]ness the Hereditary Prince Frederick Ferdinand, of Denmark."

Even over the War Department, in which Lincoln took such a direct, personal interest, the President did not exercise unrestricted authority. Secretary Stanton, who resented Lincoln's meddling in his department, ran his affairs for the most part quite independently of executive control and often in close co-operation with the anti-Lincoln Congressional Committee on the Conduct of the War. Lincoln could, of course, have removed Stanton or any other recalcitrant subordinate, but, having put up with Simon Cameron in the War Department for nearly a year, the President was reluctant to lose a secretary who might be prickly and independent-minded but who was also honest and efficient. To an impatient friend who felt Stanton had treated him unjustly, Lincoln explained his problem succinctly: "Of course I can over rule his decision if I will, but I cannot well administer the War Department independent of the Secretary of War." Indeed, instead of Lincoln's running his own War Department, it sometimes seemed that Stanton exercised a veto power upon the President. There was rueful humor in Lincoln's offhand refusal in 1862 to discuss military matters in a public speech: "The Secretary of War, you know, holds a pretty tight rein on the Press, so that they shall not tell more than they ought to, and I'm afraid that if I blab too much he might draw a tight rein on me."

Thus the same President who so drastically expanded the scope of his office by the assertion of his war powers under the Constitution was an executive who had singularly little impact either upon Congress or upon his own administrative aides. Just after his triumphant re-election in 1864, Lincoln remarked, with as much insight as wit, that he hoped he could exercise some influence with the incoming administration.

III

It is not easy to reconcile these conflicting aspects of Lincoln's presidency. The common, and kind, explanation is that the wartime President, being a very busy man, had to concentrate upon the more essential aspects of his job and to slight the others. This argument would be more convincing if Lincoln had not devoted a quite extraordinary amount of his time to really trivial matters. He found it possible, for instance, to write an endorsement of his chiropodist on the same day he issued the Emancipation Proclamation. Nor does it solve the problem to say, with Professor Corwin, that Lincoln had a "temperamental indifference to problems of administration." In certain areas such as the discovery and testing of new arms and explosives, the President exhibited a keen interest in the most routine administrative details.

Perhaps an analysis of what Lincoln himself thought about the presidency may help resolve this paradox of a Chief Executive who simultaneously expanded and abdicated his powers. For more than a quarter of a century before his first election Lincoln had vigorously participated in every presidential canvass, and his campaign speeches show that he had developed very definite ideas about the proper role of the Chief Executive. During most of this time he was a Whig, and he always remained proud of his Whig record. During the Lincoln-Douglas debates he reminded his hearers of his Whig past: "In '32, I voted for Henry Clay, in '36 for the Hugh L. White ticket, in '40 for 'Tip and Tyler.' In '44 I made the last great effort for 'Old Harry of the West.' . . . Taylor was elected in '48, and we fought nobly for Scott in '52." The leaders of the Whig party were his heroes; Henry Clay, in particular, he "loved and revered as a teacher and leader." Proud of his Whig principles, Lincoln boasted that he "had stood by the party as long as it had a being." He did not like the idea of being "un-whigged," and only after the death of his old party did he, rather reluctantly, join the Republicans.

The party to which Lincoln belonged for most of his
life originated in objections to the "executive usurpation" of Andrew Jackson. Whig leaders concealed their
economic motives and personal aspirations under de-
nunciation of Jackson as "a detestable, ignorant, reck-
less, vain and malignant tyrant." Just as their ancestors
of 1776 had stood against another executive usurper,
so the Whigs of the 1830's fought against the "dictator" in the White House. Henry Clay and Daniel
Webster bewailed the policy of the Democrats, which
was tending rapidly toward "a total change of the pure
republican character of our government, and to the
concentration of all power in the hands of one man."
William Henry Harrison, the first Whig President, made
his inaugural address a classic exposition of his party's
creed: ". . . it is preposterous to suppose that . . .
the President, placed at the capital, in the center of the
country could better understand the wants and wishes
of the people than their own immediate representatives
who spend a part of every year among them . . . and
[are] bound to them by the triple tie of interest, duty,
and affection." Zachary Taylor, the only other President elected by the Whig party, held the same views:
"The Executive . . . has authority to recommend (not
to dictate) measures to Congress. Having performed
that duty, the Executive department of the Government
cannot rightfully control the decision of Congress on
any subject of legislation . . . the . . . veto will never
be exercised by me except . . . as an extreme measure,
to be resorted to only in extraordinary cases. . . ."
    Abraham Lincoln, a young Whig campaigner who
regularly supported his party's ticket and platform,

shared these fears of a strong executive. In 1838, in one of his earliest public lectures, he expressed concern lest "some man possessed of the loftiest genius, coupled with ambition sufficient to push it to its utmost stretch," some man belonging *"to the family of the lion, or the tribe of the eagle,"* seize executive leadership and "set boldly to the task of pulling down" the institutions of the free republic. Consequently he opposed all aggrandizement of the President's powers. The Democratic tendency to allow the President "to take the whole of legislation into his own hands" he branded "a most pernicious deception." He argued against President James K. Polk's "high-handed and despotic exercise of the veto power, and . . . utter disregard of the will of the people, in refusing to give assent to measures which their representatives passed for the good and prosperity of the country." Congress should make policy and the President should execute it. That was "the best sort of principle"; that was the basic democratic "principle of allowing the people to do as they please with their own business."

These arguments were not just campaign oratory, for Lincoln clung to them throughout his life. In 1861 on his way to Washington as President Elect, he announced that he did not believe the Chief Executive should recommend legislation to Congress, veto bills already passed, or exert "indirect influence to affect the action of congress." "My political education," he declared, "strongly inclines me against a very free use of any of these means, by the Executive, to control the legislation of the country. As a rule, I think it better that congress should originate, as well as perfect its measures, without external bias." On the controversial tariff issue, for instance, he thought the President should "neither seek to force a tariff-law by Executive influence; nor yet to arrest a reasonable one, by a veto, or otherwise." Throughout the war he kept reminding his subordinates that the executive branch must not "expressly or impliedly seize and exercise the permanent legislative functions of the government."

Lincoln's curious failure to assert his control over his cabinet also derived from his basic Whig view of the presidency. The Whig party was originally founded not only to oppose executive pressures upon the Congress but to combat the President's complete domination of the administrative offices. When President Jackson abruptly removed two successive Secretaries of the Treasury in order to install a malleable third secretary who followed the President's will and removed federal deposits from the Bank of the United States, the Whigs howled that he was subjecting the entire government to *"one responsibility, one discretion, one will."* Whig President Harrison declared that the Founding Fathers should have made the head of the Treasury Department "entirely independent of the Executive," since the President should "never be looked to for schemes of finance." Other Whigs extended this reasoning to cover the rest of the cabinet. Webster was only carrying Whig principles to their logical conclusion when he asserted that all measures of an administration should be brought before the cabinet, where "their settlement was to be decided by the majority of votes, each member of the Cabinet and the President having but one vote."

Lincoln was, of course, too strong a personality to submit to such dictation. Indeed, even during the Taylor administration he had realized that the Whig theory of cabinet responsibility gave "The President the . . . ruinous character of being a mere man of straw." Consequently when Seward in April, 1861, proposed to become virtual premier of the new administration in order to lead it on a daring new policy of foreign embroilments, Lincoln quietly squelched him, declaring: ". . . if this must be done, *I* must do it." Similarly, when preparing to issue the Emancipation Proclamation, Lincoln told his cabinet advisers: "I have got you together to hear what I have written down. I do not wish your advice about the main matter — for that I have determined for myself. . . . If there is anything in the expressions I use, or in any other minor matter, which anyone of you thinks had best be changed, I shall be glad to receive the suggestions."

On key policies, therefore, especially those involving the use of the war power, Lincoln, like Harrison and Taylor before him, departed from the Whig theory of cabinet responsibility, but he could not rid himself of the political ideas with which he had been raised. Given the alternatives of imposing his own will upon his cabinet or of submitting to their majority opinion, Lincoln evaded the decision by treating the cabinet as an unnecessary nuisance, allowing it to consider only insignificant matters. Since there was no real consultation to formulate common policy and since the President could not personally oversee the details of everyday administration, each secretary, however disagreeable, self-promoting, or even conspiratorial, had a free hand in conducting his own department's affairs.

IV

These weaknesses of Lincoln's administration seem
to stand in sharp contrast with the President's energetic
assertion of his powers over civil liberties, over the military forces, and over the rebellious South, but there is
no evidence that Lincoln himself was troubled by any
inconsistency in his roles. Necessity, not political theory,
caused him to make his first sweeping assertions of executive authority during the secession crisis. The onset of
civil war posed the immediate, practical dilemma, he
declared later, "whether, using only the existing means,
agencies, and processes which Congress had provided, I
should let the government fall at once into ruin, or
whether, availing myself of the broader powers conferred
by the Constitution in cases of insurrection, I would
make an effort to save it with all its blessings for the
present age and for posterity." When the question was
so posed, the answer became simple. "Necessity knows
no law," he thought; consequently it was obligatory for
him in this crisis to take strong measures, "some of
which," he admitted, "were without any authority of
law," in order to save the government.

When it did become necessary for Lincoln to justify
his actions, he found his defense in the war powers
granted him under the Constitution. ". . . as commander-in-chief of the army and navy, in time of war,"
he asserted, "I suppose I have a right to take any measure which may best subdue the enemy." Though critics
claimed that the President was asserting dictatorial
authority, it is clear that Lincoln himself took a narrower
view of his powers. For example, he rejected the application of a general to construct a railroad in Missouri,

which, it was claimed, would have some military utility. Since real military necessity was not shown Lincoln felt this was an unwarranted extension of executive power. ". . . I have been," he assured Congress, "unwilling to go beyond the pressure of necessity in the unusual exercise of power."

The complex problem of emancipation shows the degree to which Lincoln's conception of his war powers served both as a source for executive action and as a restriction upon such action. His personal preferences, the expediencies of politics, the thundering pressure from Northern governors, and the growing sentiment that emancipation would aid the Union cause abroad all urged him during 1861 and 1862 to move against slavery. He delayed, not because he doubted his constitutional power but because he questioned the necessity. "The truth is," he told a Louisiana loyalist, "that what is done, and omitted, about slaves, is done and omitted on the same military necessity." By late 1862 when necessity clearly demanded the abolition of slavery, Lincoln issued his proclamation of freedom, "as Commander-in-Chief, of the Army and Navy of the United States in time of actual armed rebellion against authority and government of the United States, and as a fit and necessary war measure for suppressing said rebellion." The Emancipation Proclamation, he declared later, had "no constitutional or legal justification, except as a military measure."

This view that the Chief Executive possesses vast war powers is not necessarily in conflict with the Whig view of the presidency. To be sure, the Whiggish origins of Lincoln's thought on this problem are not so clearly demonstrable. The Whig party had originated in opposition to a strong President. Only two Presidents were ever elected by the Whig party, and neither of them was in the White House during time of war. Consequently, men like Webster and Clay spoke more of the limitation of presidential power in peacetime than they did of its possible wartime expansion. Lincoln himself had shared these preoccupations of his party leaders. Vigorously he denounced Democratic President Polk, who, he believed, had unjustly and unconstitutionally started the Mexican War by invading foreign territory. The argument "that if it shall become *necessary, to repel invasion,* the President, may without violation of the Constitution . . . *invade* the territory of another country" Lincoln rejected as permitting the Chief Executive "to make war at pleasure" and as subjecting the American people to "the most oppressive of all Kingly oppressions." But though he opposed the Mexican War, neither Lincoln nor his party leaders made serious objections to President Polk's vigorous assertion of his war powers once the conflict had begun.

Whigs were inhibited from making such an objection. Heirs of the Federalists, they were at heart strong nationalists. One important current of Whig thought in fact justified the broadest assertion of presidential powers in wartime. Its most articulate exponent was John Quincy Adams, who, though far too independent and cantankerous to give his undivided allegiance to any party, acted generally with the Whigs in his distinguished post-presidential career in the House of Representatives. In congressional debates in 1836, 1841, and 1842, Adams, as he proudly recorded in his diary, "stung the slaveocracy to madness" by sketching in sweeping terms the power of the President as commander-in-chief. "[B]y the laws of war," he reminded his listeners, "an invaded country has all its laws and municipal institutions swept by the board, and martial law takes the place of them." In case of "actual war, whether servile, civil, or foreign," he grimly told Congress, the South's "municipal institutions" would be entirely subject to these laws of war, which permitted the confiscation of enemy property, including slaves. Consequently, in such an event, "not only the President of the United States but the commander of the army has the power to order the universal emancipation of the slaves."

Though John Quincy Adams could never have been considered the spokesman for any party, a respectable body of Whig thinkers endorsed these views. It is significant that the strongest defender of Lincoln's power to suspend the writ of habeas corpus was the venerable Whig lawyer, Horace Binney of Philadelphia, who saw no inconsistency between this position and his condemnation of Jackson's "tyranny" during the 1830's. Another former Whig, William Whiting of Massachusetts, provided in 1862 an even broader defense of the President's powers as commander-in-chief. His booklet on *The War Powers of the President,* which went through forty-three editions during the decade after its publication, leaned heavily upon Adams' argument, which he claimed proved "in the amplest terms the powers of Congress, and the authority of the President, to free enemy's slaves, as a legitimate act of war." An old Democrat like Gideon Welles distrusted Whiting's ideas and sneered at him as "self-sufficient but superficial, with many words, some reading, but no very sound or well-founded political views," but Lincoln, who shared the lawyer's Whig background, said flatly, "I like Mr. Whiting very much . . . ," and made him Solicitor of the War Department.

Since the Whigs were generally out of office and always on the defensive, John Quincy Adams' doctrine of presidential war powers never became an official part of the party's creed, but it was not forgotten. When the Civil War came, it was the ex-Whig Horace Greeley who revived Adams' speech on the presidential power of emancipation and gave it generous space in his *New York Tribune*. Another former Whig, Senator Charles Sumner of Massachusetts, who regarded Adams' argument "as a towering landmark and beacon," welcomed the firing on Fort Sumter because it introduced just the contingency the ex-President had forecast. As soon as he heard the news, Sumner said, "I went at once to Mr. Lincoln . . . and told him I was with him now heart and soul; that under the war power the right had come to him to emancipate the slaves."

V

Thus what Lincoln called his "political education" helps explain the puzzling ambiguity of his presidency. Both in strongly asserting his war powers and in weakly deferring to Congress, he was following the Whig creed in which he was raised.

So to interpret Lincoln's course is to give more significance to the Whig party and its ideology than is fashionable among historians today. Concerned with showing that our major political parties have generally shared most of their basic ideas, recent scholars have belittled the political rivalries of the 1830's and 1840's as inconsequential struggles between conflicting economic interest groups or contests between ambitious politicians. Doubtless, in the backward glance of history, there is much justification for such an interpretation. But it must be remembered that what men think to be true often has more influence upon the course of history than actuality itself.

To the generation of American politicians who reached maturity about 1840 the difference between the Whig party and the Democratic party was a real and vital thing. Young and aspiring leaders like Abraham Lincoln who shouted themselves hoarse for rival party candidates convinced themselves, even if they convinced nobody else, that the principles which they advocated were both true and important. Rhetoric has a way of imprisoning those who use it, and the politicians of the Civil War era were never quite able to discard the party creeds of their youth. Lincoln, in other connections, recognized the danger of letting past experience dictate present action. "As our case is new," he argued, "so we must think anew, and act anew." But the President was never able to disenthrall himself from his own political education. It is ironical that the Whig party, which had a sorry record of failure during its lifetime, should have achieved its greatest success, years after its official demise, in the presidency of Abraham Lincoln.

NORMAN A. GRAEBNER

Abraham Lincoln:
CONSERVATIVE STATESMAN

Statesmanship is an illusive quality. Fundamentally it is a measure of performance, demanding nothing less than the competence and determination necessary to wield power effectively in pursuit of some conscious goal. But performance alone has never characterized true greatness, for history is strewn with the wreckage of vigorous causes that have left society worse for the effort. The arts of communication and political manipulation have worth only to the extent that they create and maintain policies which reflect both wisdom and morality. Statesmanship cannot be divorced from intelligence. It requires above all clarity of vision and recognition of man's limited political and moral means to achieve human progress. All successful statesmen of the modern world have practiced the art of the possible. Henry Clay once phrased the guiding principle of his career, "It is a rule with me, when acting in either a public or a private character, to attempt nothing more than what there exists a prospect of accomplishing."

Norman A. Graebner is a professor of history at the University of Illinois.

67

Such was the purpose and mind of Abraham Lincoln. Both as party spokesman and as President he accepted the need of dealing with things as they were, not as he would have wished them to be. Effective leadership, he believed, consisted in teaching men to accept alternatives that were always inadequate rather than creating expectations of perfection that might destroy the limited achievements that time and circumstance would permit. Let men not promise what they ought not, he once observed, lest they be called upon to perform what they cannot. Lincoln understood that men in authority, whatever the goodness of their purpose, had the primary obligation to be effective. To him it was the end result, not the principle, that mattered. "I do the very best I know how, the very best I can, and I mean to keep doing so until the end," he admitted. "If the end brings me out all right, what is said against me won't amount to anything. If the end brings me out wrong, ten angels swearing I was right would make no difference." In Lincoln's leadership was the universal appeal to reality, common sense, and expediency.

I

Lincoln accepted as the great object of his career the preservation of the remarkable legacy which the Founding Fathers had bequeathed to the nation. No generation, he said, could escape the responsibility of transmitting to the next the national edifice untrammeled and uninjured by usurpation. "This task of gratitude to our fathers, justice to ourselves, duty to posterity, and love for our species in general," he admonished, "all imperatively require us faithfully to perform." During the years that Lincoln achieved national prominence as a political leader the need of faithful performance was acute. The Union itself was in jeopardy. Its imminent destruction under the impact of the slavery issue threatened to impair the genuine promise of American democracy. As Lincoln faced the great challenge of his time in his House Divided speech of June, 1858, he called upon the country to take its bearings from the past. "If we could know where we are and whither we are tending," he said, "we could better judge what to do and how to do it."

For his stand on slavery Lincoln never claimed more than the defense of tradition. He sought to dispose of the sectional conflict and save the Union by bringing the antagonists of North and South to an acceptance of the early compromises under the Constitution. Like other conservatives of his day, Lincoln had opposed the expansionism of the Mexican War because it would "enlarge and aggravate the distracting question of slavery." Thereafter he challenged the Southern program for the expansion of slavery because it attempted to substitute the new and the untried for the proven policies of the founders of the Republic. He attacked the Kansas-Nebraska Act because its adherence to popular sovereignty disturbed the settled principle that "no line dividing local from federal authority, nor anything in the Constitution, forbade the federal government, to control as to slavery in federal territory." At Cooper Union in February, 1860, he admonished those who would extend the institution: "Not one of all your various plans can show a precedent or an advocate in the century within which our government originated. Consider, then, whether your claim of conservatism for yourselves, and your charge of destructiveness against us, are based on the most clear and stable foundations."

Nor did Lincoln ask more of the abolitionists than their adherence to the past. He shared their hatred of slavery. "If the negro is a man," he declared, "why then my ancient faith teaches me that 'all men are created equal,' and that there can be no moral right in connection with one man's making a slave of another . . . no man is good enough to govern another man without the other's consent." Slavery, Lincoln admitted to his friend Joshua Speed, in August, 1855, had the power to make him miserable. "You ought rather to appreciate," he added, "how much the great body of the Northern people do crucify their feelings, in order to maintain their loyalty to the Constitution and the Union."

If Lincoln believed slavery wrong in practice and principle, he did not share the fanaticism of the abolitionists. He was critical of slavery as an institution, but never of the South as a section. Rather he defended the South in its right to slave property so long as that property were restricted to the Southern states. "They are just what we would be in their situation," he reminded the North. "If slavery did not now exist among them, they would not introduce it. If it did now exist among us, we should not instantly give it up."

Lincoln recognized not only the South's constitutional right to slavery but also its right to the return of fugitive slaves, for even the latter rested on a long-established practice. In his Cooper Union address he summarized his appeal to the nation by asking it to accept the judgment of the past and again regard slavery "as an evil not to be extended, but to be tolerated and protected only because of and so far as its actual presence among us makes that toleration and protection a necessity. Let all the guaranties those fathers gave it be not grudgingly, but fully and fairly, maintained."

Unlike the abolitionists, Lincoln refused to condemn the South for its unwillingness to face its moral dilemma. "If all earthly power were given to me," he said at Peoria in October, 1854, "I should not know what to do, as to the existing institution." To free the slaves and deport them to Liberia would be sending them to immediate death. To free them and keep them as underlings would not improve their condition. To free them and make them political and social equals would defy the will of the great mass of white people. "Whether this feeling accords with justice and sound judgment," Lincoln advised, "is not the sole question, if indeed, it is any part of it. A universal feeling, whether well or ill-founded, cannot be safely disregarded. We cannot, then, make them equals." For Lincoln human responsibility stopped at the extremity of human power just as human responsibility began at the point where human power commenced. He recognized the essential fact that it was the racial aspect of the slavery question that tormented the nation. For this problem no one had a solution, least of all the abolitionists.

Whatever the depth of the American predicament, Lincoln knew that the nation could not long escape the obligation to resolve it. At Springfield in June, 1858, he reminded his audience that the slavery agitation had been increasing steadily. Nor would it cease, he warned, "until a *crisis* shall have been reached, and passed. 'A house divided against itself cannot stand.' I believe this government cannot endure, permanently *half slave* and *half free*. I do not expect the Union to be dissolved — I do not expect the house to fall — but I do expect it will cease to be divided. It will become *all* one thing, or *all* the other." This was not a declaration of war; it was a statement of fact. Lincoln more than any other man of his generation saw that the United States would be forced one day to face the question of slavery without equivocation. Unless slavery were limited and controlled by federal action, it would either triumph totally or be totally uprooted. Defending his House Divided speech Lincoln phrased his program for disposing of the slavery question:

I have declared a thousand times, and now repeat that, in my opinion, neither the General Government, nor any other power outside of the slave states, can constitutionally or rightfully interfere with slaves or slavery where it already exists. I believe that whenever the effort to spread slavery into the New Territories, by whatever means, and into the free States themselves, by Supreme Court decisions, shall be fairly headed off, the institution will then be in course of ultimate extinction. . . .

Lincoln's response to the Southern independence movement reflected a deep-seated realism. Secession was wrong because it was unconstitutional; it was intolerable because it was destructive of the Union. But Lincoln did not condemn the secessionist movement as immoral. He understood that appeals to righteousness were far less effective than appeals to power. He merely warned the South that it could not dissolve the Union. "With the purse and sword, the army and navy and treasury in our hands and at our command," he admonished the South in 1856, "you *couldn't do it*. . . . All this talk about the dissolution of the Union is humbug — nothing but folly. *We won't* dissolve the Union, and *you shan't*." At Cincinnati in September, 1859, Lincoln conceded that man for man the North had no advantage over the South, but he added pointedly, "there are not so many of you as there are of us . . . being inferior in numbers, you will make nothing by attempting to master us."

With that same disturbing grasp of reality Lincoln chided the South for its intolerance of the Republican Party. Nothing that the South could do, he observed, would quiet the Northern conscience. Antislavery sentiment, he reminded his Southern opponents during the election year of 1860, already commanded a million and a half votes. That sentiment would not be destroyed by breaking up the party which gave it expression. To force it outside the peaceful channel of the democratic process would augment rather than diminish the number of John Browns in the nation. Nor was there any escape from the relentless pressure of freesoilism, he warned, in the legalistic argumentation of the Dred Scott decision.

Lincoln reassured Alexander H. Stephens of Georgia in December, 1860, that he would not interfere with slavery where it enjoyed the defense of the Constitution. In that respect the South had no more to fear than it did in the days of Washington. But one great difference remained and it left no room for compromise. "You think slavery is right and ought to be extended," he wrote, "while we think it is wrong and ought to be restricted. That, I suppose, is the rub." Not even war,

Lincoln declared finally, would permit the South to elude the challenges of Northern power, economic preponderance, or moral sentiment. Physically speaking, the sections could not separate. "Suppose you go to war," he asked the South in his First Inaugural Address, "you cannot fight always; and when, after much loss on both sides, and no gain on either, you cease fighting, the identical old questions as to terms of intercourse are again upon you." Only by returning to the decisions of the past, Lincoln warned the nation with relentless argumentation, would it avoid the hard penalty of civil conflict.

II

Lincoln accepted the war imposed upon him by the bombardment of Fort Sumter, for he was now convinced that only through struggle could America be restored to its own traditions. From external attack the democratic experiment appeared secure. Lincoln himself had written as early as 1838: "If destruction be our lot, we must ourselves be its author and finisher. As a nation of freemen, we must live through all time, or die by suicide." Now the nation faced the challenge of a massive effort to destroy it from within. The great issue in conflict, Lincoln saw, was whether a minority of discontented individuals could, without any legal pretence, break up their government and endanger the very concept of free institutions upon the earth. "Is there," he asked, "in all republics, this inherent, and fatal weakness? Must a government, of necessity, be too *strong* for the liberties of its own people, or too *weak* to maintain its own existence?" American democracy had the obligation to demonstrate to the world that those who won fairly through the ballot could suppress those who resorted to bullets. "Such," he said three months after Sumter, "will be a great lesson of peace: teaching men that what they cannot take by an election, neither can they take by a war; teaching all the folly of being the beginners of a war."

As wartime President, Lincoln demonstrated that the niceties of life are less essential than stamina in the great moments of history. He took on his own conscience, and his conscience alone, the burden of the war. He accepted the responsibility for its destruction and ordered his fellowmen killed without apology. He made the hard decisions, whatever the sacrifices they entailed or the weight they placed on those who carried the military burden. He wielded power without regret, for he knew that only through victory over Southern arms could he achieve the restoration of the past. He encouraged his generals to pursue the war with vigor. Seldom had the modern world witnessed such battles as Antietam, Cold Harbor, and Fredericksburg. Gradually the war became total with all its horrors, pillage, and destruction. "I send out parties of cavalry here & there, and instruct men coolly to burn, kill and destroy," admitted one officer engaged in fighting guerrillas in Missouri. Devastation mounted with the progress of war, for by such methods alone would the South be brought to its knees.

Many in the North condemned Lincoln for his willingness to employ force against the South. During the early months of the war he reminded his pacifist critics of his obligation to defend the North against Southern aggression. To a delegation representing the YMCA association of Baltimore he declared in April, 1861: "You express great horror of bloodshed, and yet you would not lay a straw in the way of those who are organizing in Virginia and elsewhere to capture this city. The rebels attack Fort Sumter, and your citizens attack troops sent to the defense of the government . . . and yet you would have me break my oath and surrender the government without a blow. There is no Washington in that — no Jackson in that — no manhood nor honor in that."

Lincoln answered those who censured his later conduct of the war that the only alternatives to the suppression of the rebellion by force of arms were either conceding the Union or agreeing to some compromise settlement with the South. But, he added, there was no compromise possible which would embrace a Southern acceptance of the Union. The strength of the rebellion was in the Confederate Army, and no compromise proposal by the South would have effect unless the military leaders agreed to it. Any effort at a settlement before the South had been liberated from the domination of its military forces, Lincoln warned, would waste time and improve the advantage of the enemy. Throughout the war he insisted that any departure from his military policies would insure the success of the rebellion. "This is not a question of sentiment or taste," he said, "but one of physical force which may be measured and estimated as horsepower and steam power are measured and estimated. Keep it and you can save the Union. Throw it away, and the Union goes with it."

Lincoln's war aims were clear. He would be content, he told a Trenton audience in February, 1861, if he could be the humble instrument of the Almighty in preserving what the Founding Fathers had created — national independence, the Union, the Constitution, and the liberty of the American people. If Lincoln would restore the past, however, it had to be the past as he understood it. War had come because the South had preferred secession to any acceptance of what he believed to be the American tradition on matters of slavery — that it was evil and ought to be restricted. The South had extracted too high a price for peace. But having resorted to war, never again would it enjoy peace on its own terms. "This government cannot much longer play a game in which it stakes all, and its enemies stake nothing," he wrote in July, 1862. "Those enemies must understand that they cannot experiment for ten years trying to destroy the government, and if they fail still come back into the Union unhurt." The reforged Union would be responsible to its democratic creed that all men are created equal. "On the side of the Union," he wrote, "it is a struggle for maintaining in the world that form and substance of government whose leading object is to elevate the condition of man; to lift artificial weights from all shoulders; to clear the paths of laudable pursuits for all; to afford all an unfettered start and a fair chance in the race for life." The South could escape the war only with slavery restricted and on the road to oblivion.

War for Lincoln was always a means, not an end. Whether it would accomplish any lasting good commensurate with its terrible cost would be the supreme measure of Lincoln's statesmanship. He pursued the war, but he never promised the American people more than war could achieve. He understood that Northern power was limited and that the objects of war had to conform to that limited power. He sought only to assure the nation that if his goals were restricted they were still worthy of the effort and cost of war. It was essential that the spilling of blood not be in vain. Restoration of the Union, Lincoln believed, was the one estimable goal that Northern power could achieve. "I must save this government if possible," he wrote. "What I *cannot* do, of course I *will* not do, but it may as well be understood, once for all, that I shall not surrender this game leaving any available card unplayed." In the midst of the war's fury he wrote, "I would save the Union. I would save it the shortest way under the Constitution. The sooner the national authority can be restored, the nearer the Union will be to the Union as it was. . . . My paramount object in this struggle is to save the Union."

It was to this task that Lincoln committed the North, for even this limited goal would require its best efforts. "Fellow-citizens," he addressed Congress in his December message of 1862, "we cannot escape history. We of this Congress and this administration will be remembered in spite of ourselves. No personal significance, or insignificance, can spare one or another of us. The fiery trial through which we pass, will light us down, in honor or dishonor, to the latest generation. We *say* we are for the Union. The world will not forget that we say this. We know how to save the Union. The world knows we do know how to save it. We — even *we here* — hold the power, and bear the responsibility."

III

For Republican Radicals, stimulated by abolitionism and the bitter emotions of war, Lincoln's goals were far too restrained. These men demanded that he secure no less than a revolution in Southern society. To them it was incongruous to fight the war to victory without up-rooting slavery and with it the slaveholding class. They accused Lincoln of lacking all concern for humanity. Many who before secession had refused to attack the institution of slavery now demanded abolition as a means of ending the war. Thaddeus Stevens urged Lincoln to pursue the war without quarter, arming the slaves against their masters. Republicans would learn, he warned, that eventually they would be forced to treat the seceding states as conquered provinces and drive the rebels into exile. "They have such determination, energy, and endurance," he cried, "that nothing but actual ex-termination or exile or starvation will ever induce them to surrender to this government."

Following the Democratic victories in the elections of 1862 which reduced the Republican majority in the House from 35 to 18, the pressure on Lincoln mounted. Northern editors and politicians chanted for a change in policy and in cabinet personnel. Now the destruction of the South had a political as well as a humanitarian ob-jective. To win the war without destroying the planter class would permit the rebellious leaders to reorganize the South and dispatch their own delegations to Con-gress. These, with the pro-slavery conservatives of the border states and the Northern Democrats, would reduce the Republican Party and Republican principles to a minority status. Lincoln could satisfy the needs of hu-manity (and of the Republican Party) only by altering the nature and the purpose of the war.

Freedom for all Americans was a great moral end.

But Lincoln knew that freedom was an abstraction that was subject to varying interpretations. For some, liberty meant that each man could do as he pleased; for others, it meant that each man could do as he pleased with other men. "The shepherd drives the wolf from the sheep's throat," said Lincoln with uncanny wisdom, "for which the sheep thanks the shepherd as a *liberator,* while the wolf denounces him for the same act as the destroyer of liberty. . . ." These differences in attitude, Lincoln added, existed in the North where all professed to love liberty. Great changes in any society would always be hailed by some as an advance of liberty and bewailed by others as the destruction of liberty. Lincoln saw that the noble purpose of liberation must still be limited by the complexities of the problems that always follow the freeing of peoples.

Lincoln recognized the limited efficacy of men to create a heaven on earth. Unlike the abolitionists, he refused to use power to create change unmindful of the greater damage which might ensue. He once said that he "would consent to any *great* evil, to avoid a *greater* one." Lincoln was no believer in doctrines, for he knew that they destroyed reason and betrayed man against himself. To him they were "pernicious abstractions." He regarded abstract ideals as an abomination to statecraft, for they created objectives that seldom had any relation to specific interests at stake. They were no guide for action because they were never limited by the realities of power.

Lincoln harbored a pessimistic view of man and society. He often recalled with pride the achievements of popular government in America. That the experiment in democracy had not failed was obvious everywhere. "Look at it," he said, "in its aggregate grandeur, of extent of country, the numbers of population — of ship, and steamboat, and rail. . . ." Lincoln's sympathy for the underdog, his awareness of social needs, his enthusiasm for democracy, and his adherence to the Declaration of Independence have led many historians to regard Lincoln as a liberal. But there was a marked ambivalence in his liberalism. He doubted that human society could ever approach utopia, for its maladjustments mirrored the general frailty and depravity of mankind. Force would always remain a necessity to maintain a balance among individuals and groups suspended in a world of conflicting interests. Reminiscent of the *Federalist* Lincoln once observed that "if all men were just, there still would be *some,* though not *so much,* need of government."

Lincoln doubted that the world would be made much better because he had once occupied a position of great authority. His spirit was not that of a crusader. He confessed near the end of his life that he had not controlled events, but that events had controlled him. This humble view of his role in history reflected Lincoln's absolute doubt that Providence spoke through him, or that he grasped all truth or possessed all virtue. He experienced no compulsion to guide the destiny of man toward some earthly paradise. If a fanatic often cannot distinguish his own voice from the voice of God, Lincoln was sure that his was not the voice of God. In any great struggle, he recalled, each side claimed to act in accordance with divine will. "Both *may* be, and one *must* be wrong," ran his deduction. He promised only that he would follow the will of Providence if he could ever discover it. "These are not . . . the days of miracles," he admitted ruefully, "and I suppose it will be granted that I am not to expect a direct revelation. I must study the plain physical facts of the case, ascertain what is possible and learn what appears to be wise and right." If Lincoln brought great good to the Republic, it was precisely because he was not quite sure that he could.

Lincoln was a man of reflection; his presidential career was characterized by vast silences. William H. Herndon once said of him that "he read less and thought more than any man in his sphere in America." Lincoln had a feeling for the pace of history. His close friend, Leonard Swett, believed that he succeeded in politics by ignoring small events and calculating closely the major trends of the age. "The whole world to him," wrote Swett, "was a question of cause and effect. He believed the results to which certain causes tended; he did not believe that those results could be materially hastened or impeded." Lincoln maneuvered so that events found him in the right place. Seldom has a man who wielded power in such momentous times revealed such conservative habits of thought.

Lincoln refused to attribute any unique depravity to the South; nor would he insist that Southerners deny any special guilt by taking an oath that they had done no wrong. This, he said, "rejects the Christian principle of forgiveness in terms of repentence. I think it is enough if the man does no wrong *hereafter*." To expect men to react favorably to moral condemnation was, thought Lincoln, "to expect a reversal of human nature, which is God's decree, and never can be reversed." He warned that any effort to dictate to a man's judgment or to shun and despise him for his alleged evil would merely cause him to retreat within himself and close all avenues to his mind. Lincoln added that "tho' your cause be naked truth itself, transformed to the heaviest lance . . . and tho' you throw it with more than Herculean force and precision, you shall no more be able to pierce him, than to penetrate the hard shell of a tortoise with a rye straw. Such is man, and so *must* he be understood by those who would lead him, even to his own best interest."

Lincoln denied that the problems of society would be cured by inflicting notions of perfection on others. "When the conduct of men is designed to be influenced," he wrote, *"persuasion,* kind, unassuming persuasion, should ever be adopted." To turn men adrift, to condemn them without remedy, so that good may abound, he added, was "something so repugnant to humanity, so uncharitable, so cold-blooded and feelingless, that it never did, nor ever can enlist the enthusiasm of a popular cause. . . . The generous man could not adopt it. It could not mix with his blood." Lincoln would mitigate man's inhumanity, not through moral crusades, but through tolerance and magnanimity. "Important principles," he once said, "may and must be flexible."

Lincoln's conservatism ruled out a war for righteousness. Radical goals, he feared, would overreach Northern power. They would merely reduce the struggle to endless and hopeless destruction. Lincoln's primary concern was for the future. In his appeal to the border states in May, 1862, to adopt gradual emancipation, he reminded them that their decision must consider the centuries to come. "May the vast future," he said, "not have to lament that you have neglected it." He resisted immediate abolition from fear that extended evil would result from a sudden derangement in the status of the Southern Negroes. He doubted that the future of the Negro in the South would be resolved by the good intentions of men of the North. Whatever the destruction of the South and its military power, the Southern whites would continue to possess the social, economic, and political power over the Negro whether he were slave or free.

Lincoln's reluctance to destroy slavery through war stemmed partially from his constitutional and legal scruples. His oath, he insisted, forbade him from indulging his abstract judgment of the slavery question. Lincoln had a conservative devotion to law and order. He condemned all disrespect for property. Let every man remember, he warned early in his career, that "to violate the law, is to trample on the blood of his father, and to tear the charter of his own, and his children's liberty. Let reverence for the laws . . . become the *political religion* of the nation; and let the old and the young, the rich and the poor, the grave and the gay, of all sexes and tongues, and colors and conditions, sacrifice unceasingly upon its altars. . . ." He reminded Congress in December, 1862, that the liberation of the slaves was the destruction of property, acquired by purchase or inheritance as any other property. Nor was the South any more responsible than the North for its original introduction into North America or for its continuance. Did not the North unhesitantly purchase and share the profits of cotton and sugar?

Thus Lincoln's appeal had little in common with that

of the Radicals. His famous reply to the moralist, Horace Greeley, in August, 1862, was eloquent in its realism:

My paramount object in this struggle is to save the Union, and is *not* either to save or to destroy slavery. If I could save the Union without freeing *any* slave, I would do it, and if I could save it by freeing *all* the slaves, I would do it; and if I could save it by freeing some and leaving others alone I would also do that. What I do about slavery, and the coloured race, I do because I believe it helps to save the Union; and what I forbear, I forbear because I do *not* believe it would help to save the Union. I shall do *less* whenever I shall believe that what I am doing hurts the cause, and I shall do *more* whenever I shall believe doing more will help the cause.

Lincoln's action was moral whereas John Brown's was not, because Lincoln measured the extent of Northern capability to do good for the Negroes of the South and because he was ever mindful of consequences.

Lincoln accepted emancipation only when it appeared the necessary price for Union. Liberation, he knew, was no panacea. It could not dispose of the great social problems of the South. But if it would unite the North behind the primary goal of Union, it would be worth the cost. "It had got to be midsummer, 1862," Lincoln recalled later. "Things had gone on from bad to worse, until I felt that we had reached the end of our rope on the plan of operations we had been pursuing; that we had about played our last card, and must change our tactics, or lose the game! I now determined upon the adoption of the emancipation policy. . . ." The Union always came first. When one soldier complained to the

President that he would not fight to free Negroes, Lincoln replied, "Fight you, then, exclusively to save the Union. I issued the proclamation on purpose to aid you in saving the Union. Whenever you shall have conquered all resistance to the Union, if I shall urge you to continue fighting, it will be apt time, then, for you to declare you will not fight to free Negroes." Lincoln permitted no one to confuse the issues of the war.

IV

Nowhere did Lincoln reveal his conservative instincts more clearly than in his foreign relations. No American President has illustrated with greater precision the only viable relationship between idealism and realism in the conduct of diplomacy. Throughout the decade of the fifties American idealism had burned brightly as it reached out to all the world. Said Ralph Waldo Emerson of this country's obligation to humanity: "The office of America is to liberate, to abolish kingcraft, priestcraft, caste, monopoly, to pull down the gallows, to burn up the bloody statute book, to take in the immigrant, to open the doors of the sea and the fields of the earth. . . ." Lewis Cass, the noted Michigan Democrat, promised a New York audience in 1852 that America's democratic voice would one day control the destiny of all nations. "I trust the time will soon come," he cried, "when not a hostile drum shall roll, and not a hostile cannon be fired, throughout the world, if we say, 'Your cause is not a just and right one.' "

Nor had Lincoln escaped the liberating sentiment of the age. When Louis Kossuth, the defiant Hungarian liberal, led his people to a declaration of independence from Austrian Hapsburg rule in April, 1849, a sympathetic meeting was held in Springfield, Illinois. Lincoln reported the resolutions which extended to the revolting Hungarians this nation's "warmest sympathy" and "most ardent prayers for their speedy triumph and final success." The revolution failed, but three years later another Springfield meeting declared that "the sympathies of this country, and the benefits of its position, should be exerted in favor of the people of every nation struggling to be free. . . ." In his eulogy to Henry Clay, delivered in the Illinois State House in 1852, Lincoln said: "Mr Clay's predominant sentiment, from first to last, was a deep devotion to the cause of human liberty — a strong sympathy for the oppressed everywhere, and an ardent wish for their elevation."

Lincoln's idealism toward the world beyond the nation's borders did not falter when he assumed responsibility for American foreign policy. But it was an idealism that transcended mere declarations of moral purpose. The collapse of the independence movements in Europe illustrated the limited efficacy of statements of righteous intent that embraced everything and came to grips with nothing. For Lincoln America's contribution to human progress would be limited largely to example. The nation would fulfill its obligation to humanity by being true to itself. At Peoria in October, 1854, he expressed his apprehension "that the one retrograde institution in America, is undermining the principle of progress, and fatally violating the noblest political system the world ever saw." Shortly after the outbreak of war in 1861 he declared to John Hay that the central theme of the struggle was the necessity of proving to the world that popular government was not an absurdity. His message to Congress in July, 1861, pointed out that the outcome of the war involved more than the fate of the United States. It embraced, he said, "the whole family of man." Urging the nation to accept the burden of reforging the Union in December, 1862, he declared in cosmic terms, "We shall nobly save or meanly lose the last, best hope of earth." At Gettysburg he again placed the American experiment in its world setting. He paid tribute to the dead, but added the imperative obligation that the nation strive on so that the cause for which they fought should not perish from the earth.

Lincoln avoided moral commitments that he knew American power could not fulfill. Early in 1863 Polish revolutionists made an heroic effort to throw off the tyranny of the Czar. The French government, under Napoleon III, sent an appeal to the United States for support in exerting "a moral influence on the Emperor of Russia." Secretary of State William H. Seward responded for the Lincoln administration. In a letter to the French minister of May 11, 1863, Seward acknowledged the American interest in public order and humanity. But he added positively: "Notwithstanding . . . the favor with which we thus regard the suggestion of the Emperor of the French, this government finds an insurmountable difficulty in the way of any active cooperation with the governments of France, Austria, and Great Britain. . . ."

Seward admitted that American democratic idealism had attracted the attention of revolutionists of every country in their search for sympathy if not active support. But the American nation, he said, preferred to yield to the counsels of President Washington that "the American people must be content to recommend the course of human progress by the wisdom with which they should exercise the powers of self-government, forbearing at all time, and in every way, from foreign alliances, intervention, and interference." There had been many "seductions," he admitted, to involve the United States in events abroad, such as the Hungarian revolution, but each appeal had been disallowed by the American government. "Our policy of non-intervention, straight, absolute, and peculiar as it may seem to other nations," he added, "has become a traditional one, which could not be abandoned without the most urgent occasion, amounting to a manifest necessity. . . ." If the United States had good wishes for the progress of humanity in Europe, the nation's policy of nonintervention was not without advantage to the interests of mankind. Lincoln and Seward distinguished clearly between moral obligation and the national interest.

Lincoln anchored his foreign policy to a realistic judgment of power. This accounts for the astonishing equanimity with which he responded to Napoleon's threatened intervention of Mexico in 1862. In sharp contrast to many of the nation's excited editors and politicians, he understood that the Monroe Doctrine was a viable and defensible American commitment not because of its idealistic appeal to liberty and self-determination but because it was an accurate reflection of New World power. He refused to involve the United States in a moral commitment by appealing to the doctrine. Instead, he warned Napoleon that France could not establish a monarchy in Mexico because the Mexicans would not permit it. Wrote Seward to the French government in March, 1862: "The President . . . deems it his duty to express . . . in all candor and frankness, the opinion that no monarchial government which could be founded in Mexico, in the presence of foreign navies and armies . . . would have any prospect of security or permanency. Secondly, that the instability of such a monarchy there would be enhanced if the throne should be assigned to any person not of Mexican nativity. That under such circumstances the new government must speedily fall unless it could draw into its support European alliances, which . . . would be the beginning rather than the ending of revolution in Mexico." This warning, the secretary added, was grounded on some knowledge of the political sentiments and habits of society in America.

Lincoln saw that the freedom of the Western Hemisphere from European control had dominated the history of the preceding century. Europe would not succeed in reversing that trend while the population and resources of the Americas continued their steady development. It was doubtful also, Seward chided the French, that the nations of Europe would ever agree on any policy favorable to a counterrevolution, for their interests were too diverse. Even when France established Maximilian of Austria as the Emperor of Mexico Seward continued to avoid any open American commitment to Mexican independence. When, at the close of the Civil War, General Ulysses S. Grant urged an immediate campaign into Mexico, Seward opposed him. The Empire, he said, was crumbling, and the whole episode would be over in six months and perhaps as little as sixty days. Lincoln refused to become involved in any war that was of no vital interest to the nation. He recognized the need of hoarding the country's energy to preserve the Union, and he refused to dissipate American resources in needless involvements abroad to defend principles which must succeed or fail on their own. As the American minister in Paris, John Bigelow, wrote in the spring of 1865, the administration would not fight to restore Republican government in Mexico. He added succinctly, "Whoever thinks the contrary, I fear, is deceived."

V

With the assurance after 1863 of an ultimate Northern triumph over the South, Lincoln saw that the Union hinged less on Northern power than on the willingness of the American people to live together in peace and co-operation. For him the war was always a struggle within one civilization, not a crusade of humanity against barbarism. To restore unity to American civilization he dared not weaken the bonds of affection irreparably by using power merely to chastise and eradicate. Lincoln agreed with Greeley that a country cannot be held together with bayonets. If force could remove the obstacles to reunion, it could perform only half the task. What remained could be achieved only by generosity and forgiveness.

Lincoln's final policy toward the South was characterized by a necessary dichotomy. He employed all power at hand to destroy the Confederate Army but attempted simultaneously to sweeten Southern bitterness at the defeat of its cause. In his First Inaugural Address he appealed to the common memories of North and

South, stretching, he said, "from every battlefield and patriot grave to every living heart and hearthstone all over this broad land. . . ." To reconstruct the Union spiritually as well as physically was Lincoln's central object during the final year of the war. Beginning with his message to Congress in December, 1863, he promised amnesty to all participants in the rebellion, with some exceptions, who would swear allegiance to the Constitution and the Union and accept the existing decrees regarding slavery. Whenever one-tenth the number who voted in 1860 had taken the oath and established a state government, that state could resume its position in the Union. Lincoln clung to this program until his death. With his veto of the Radical Wade-Davis bill of 1864, he reaffirmed his determination to control all policy toward the South. "If they choose to make a point upon this," he said of the Radicals, "I do not doubt that they can do harm. They have never been friendly to me. At all events, I must bear some consciousness of being somewhere near right. I must keep some standard of principle fixed within myself."

In December, 1864, Lincoln announced to the South that it could have peace as soon as it laid down its arms. Whatever questions remained could be settled by peaceful means. In his Second Inaugural Address he promised to do nothing through malice, for only through charity could the work of Union be accomplished. Less than a month later Lincoln met with Generals Grant and Sherman and announced that he was prepared for the civil reorganization of the South and the extension of rights to Southerners as citizens of a common country. Already he had come to the hard realization that victory over the South would merely shift the issue of the Union from the field of battle to the halls of Congress. His last speech of April 11, 1865, was directed at the North to accept his purpose of peace without recrimination. He emphasized again the need of bringing the Southern states into "their proper practical relation with the Union" without delay.

On the day of his assassination, Lincoln called the attention of his cabinet to the vengeful spirit rampant among the Radicals. He warned that he would oppose it: "I hope there will be no persecutions, no bloody work after the war is over. No one need to expect me to take part in hanging or killing their men, even the worst of them. Enough lives have been sacrificed; we must extinguish our resentments if we expect harmony and Union. There is too much desire on the part of some of our very good friends to be masters, to interfere and dictate to those states, to treat people not as fellow citizens; there is too little respect for their rights. I do not sympathize in these." Lincoln's final admonition proved to be no chart for the future, for within a day he was dead. Andrew Johnson, his successor, was no match for the rapacity of the Radicals whose revolutionary purpose of creating a new, industrial America rather than returning to the past demanded a continuing cold war against the South. Lincoln reforged the Union, but it was not to be the Union that he had known.

Lincoln's contribution to the nation was immeasurable. Despite the emotions of great crisis, he never permitted a crusading zeal to blur his goals or force him to accept obligations beyond the power which he wielded. His deep conservatism forbade any concession to the demands of the ideologues around him. He saw that power could achieve only limited good and that any effort to employ force as if it could alter the fundamental nature of human society might produce disaster. His attitudes toward France, the Polish repression, slavery, and the Union were characterized by a persistent realism, for he doubted that the Republic could bring genuine freedom to all its own citizens, much less to the people of Europe. As a leader in wartime Lincoln demonstrated that limited goals are still compatible with democracy and total war; that force to achieve any good commensurate with its cost must be tempered with fairness, justice, and tolerance; and that war fought with reason can, if it must come, attain the fulfillment of decent and humane objectives.

AN

EXHIBIT

OF

MATERIALS

ON DISPLAY

IN THE

UNIVERSITY

OF ILLINOIS

LIBRARY

DURING

FEBRUARY

1959

THE ENDURING LINCOLN

SELECTED

AND

DESCRIBED

BY

LESLIE

W.

DUNLAP

THE ENDURING LINCOLN

This exhibit of writings by and about Abraham Lincoln, on display at the University of Illinois Library during February, 1959, is designed to show certain aspects of his life and career which are worthy of study one hundred and fifty years after his birth on February 12, 1809.

Three books published in the present decade should be read and reread by the student who wishes to become acquainted with "The Enduring Lincoln."

. . . .

1. Thomas, Benjamin P., *Abraham Lincoln, a Biography.* New York: Knopf, 1952. 548 p.

   This brief and masterful work probably is the best introduction to the life of Lincoln.

   One of 500 copies printed on rag paper and signed by the author.

. . . .

2. *The Living Lincoln: The Man, His Mind, His Times, and The War He Fought, Reconstructed from His Own Writings.* Edited by Paul M. Angle

and Earl Schenck Miers. New Brunswick, N. J.: Rutgers University Press, 1955. 673 p.

The Living Lincoln, the best selection of Lincoln's letters and speeches in one volume, follows the texts and notes of *The Collected Works of Abraham Lincoln* published in 1953 in nine volumes.

· · · · · · · · ·

3. Sandburg, Carl, *Abraham Lincoln: The Prairie Years and The War Years.* One-Volume Edition. New York: Harcourt, Brace [c1954].

The author characterizes this work as "a distillation" of his biography of Lincoln in six volumes.

One of ten copies specially bound for the publishers in two volumes.

I. His Appearance

Although photography was not invented until Lincoln had reached the age of thirty, his photographers (in particular, Alexander Hesler of Chicago, and Mathew B. Brady and Alexander Bardner of Washington) left a splendid record of his features. The work of these early camera men helped to make the face of Lincoln one of the "best-known faces in the whole world." (David Lloyd George, *International Conciliation,* No. 156 (November, 1920), p. 21.)

· · · · · · · · ·

4. Meserve, Frederick Hill, *The Photographs of Abraham Lincoln.* New York: Privately printed, 1911. 110 p. Supplements published in 1917, 1938, 1950, and 1955.

"The features and form of Lincoln are well known,

for he was perhaps the most photographed man of his time. Yet there are only about one hundred different photographic portraits still existing, all but two or three of which were made during the last eight years of his life, after he had become of national importance." [p. 21]

The four Supplements contain thirty additional photographs.

Copy No. 27 of an edition of 102 numbered and signed copies.

. . . .

5. Lorant, Stefan, "A Pictorial Bibliography," in *Lincoln, a Picture Story of His Life.* Revised and enlarged edition. (New York: Harper [c1957].) Pp. 274-298.

"A careful examination of the pictures [in F. H. Meserve's *The Photographs of Abraham Lincoln* and supplements] shows that some of the 'different' photographs listed under different numbers are not different at all, but one and the same." [p. 275]

"To sum up: the Meserve list of 132 items should be reduced by 30. Our pictorial bibliography numbers 102 Lincoln photographs, an addition of 2 since the last edition [1952]." [p. 277]

. . . .

DESCRIPTIONS

6. *Abraham Lincoln's AUTOBIOGRAPHY, with an Account of Its Origin and History and Additional Biographical Material.* Edited by Robert Dale Richardson. Boston: Beacon Press, 1947. 45 p.

"If any personal description of me is thought desirable,

it may be said, I am, in height, six feet, four inches, nearly; lean in flesh, weighing, on an average, one hundred and eighty pounds; dark complexion with coarse black hair, and grey eyes — No other marks or brands recollected." [p. 26]

The manuscript is in the Library of Congress.

· · · · · · · · ·

7. Whitman, Walt, Washington, to Nat and Fred Gray, March 19, 1863. As quoted in *The Magazine of History with Notes and Queries,* XXI (1922), Extra Number 81, p. 15.

"I think Well of the President. He has a face like a Hoosier Michael Angelo, so awful ugly it becomes beautiful, with its strange mouth, its deep-cut criss-cross lines and its doughnut complexion." [p. 5]

· · · · · · · · ·

8. Herndon, William H., and Jesse William Weik, *Herndon's Lincoln, the True Story of a Great Life.* Chicago: Belford, Clarke [c1889]. 3 v.

"Thus, I repeat, stood and walked and talked this singular man. He was odd, but when that gray eye and that face and those features were lit up by the inward soul in fires of emotion, then it was that all those apparently ugly features sprang into organs of beauty or disappeared in the sea of inspiration that often flooded his face. Sometimes it appeared as if Lincoln's soul was fresh from its creator." [III, p. 590]

Chapter XX (III, pp. 582-611) is the classic descrip-tion of the mature Lincoln in Springfield.

9. Hay, John, "Life in the White House in the Time of Lincoln," *The Century Magazine,* XLI (November, 1890), pp. 33-37.

"As time wore on and the war held its terrible course, upon no one of all those who lived through it was its effect more apparent than upon the President. . . . Under this frightful ordeal his demeanor and disposition changed — . . . He continued always the same kindly, genial, and cordial spirit he had been at first; but the boisterous laughter became less frequent year by year; the eye grew veiled by constant meditation on momentous subjects; the air of reserve and detachment from his surroundings increased. He aged with great rapidity." [pp. 36-37]

. . . .

10. Nicolay, John G., "Lincoln's Personal Appearance," *The Century Magazine,* XLII (October 1891), pp. 932-938.

"Graphic art was powerless before a face that moved through a thousand delicate gradations of line and contour, light and shade, sparkle of the eye and curve of the lip, in the long gamut of expression from grave to gay, and back again from the rollicking jollity of laughter to that serious, far-away look that with prophetic intuitions beheld the awful panorama of war, and heard the cry of oppression and suffering. There are many pictures of Lincoln; there is no portrait of him." [p. 933]

. . . .

11. Sandburg, Carl, "The Face of Lincoln," in Frederick Hill Meserve and Carl Sandburg, *The*

Photographs of Abraham Lincoln. (New York: Harcourt, Brace [c1944].) Pp. 1-16.

"Artists and sculptors, many painters and illustrators, common people of whom the Lord made many, have spoken of the fascination and the profound involvements to be seen in the face and physical form of Abraham Lincoln. The exterior man moved with some of the mystery of the interior man." [p. 1]

II. The Man

Probably the most fascinating aspect of the study of Lincoln is his personality, a blend of lights and shadows which dazzles beholders and baffles description.

. . . .

12. William H. Herndon to Ward Hill Lamon, February 25, 1870. As quoted in David Donald, *Lincoln's Herndon.* Introduction by Carl Sandburg. (New York: Knopf, 1948.) P. 302.

"He was so good & so odd a man, how in the hell could I help study him."

. . . .

13. Ingersoll, Robert G., *Abraham Lincoln, a Lecture.* New York: C. P. Farrell, 1895. 53 p.

"*ABRAHAM LINCOLN* — strange mingling of mirth and tears, of the tragic and grotesque, of cap and crown, of Socrates and Democritus, of AEsop and Marcus Aurelius, of all that is gentle and just, humorous and honest, merciful, wise, laughable, lovable and divine, and all consecrated to the use of man . . ." [p. 43]

Ingersoll set a pattern for characterizations of Lincoln.

14. Newton, Joseph Fort, *Lincoln and Herndon*. Cedar Rapids, Iowa: The Torch Press, 1910. 367 p.

"One who follows Lincoln down the years, from a windowless log cabin to the White House, does not find it easy to write about him calmly. He was a man of such high and tender humanity, of personality so appealing and pathos so melting, that almost every study of him ends in a blur of eulogy. . . .

"There is a certain mystery about Lincoln, as there is about every great and simple man; a mystery too simple, it may be, to be found out." [p. 333]

. . . .

15. Nicolay, Helen, *Personal Traits of Abraham Lincoln*. New York: Century, 1912. 387 p.

"A man of many moods but great singleness of aim, he was complex, yet of a strange simplicity. . . . Humble-minded, he was confident of his own powers. Intensely practical, he was dowered with a poet's vision, and a poet's capacity for pain. Keen, analytical, absolutely just, he was affectionate — and tender-hearted almost to the verge of unreason. Fond of merriment, he was one of the saddest men who ever lived." [pp. 10-11]

. . . .

16. Barnard, George Grey, "The Sculptor's View of Lincoln," in *Barnards's Lincoln*. (Cincinnati: Stewart and Kidd, 1917.) Pp. 21-30.

"Lincoln stands for clearness, for knowledge. He deals simply with the facts of life, helps his neighbors in their homely tasks, laughs with them. There is mystery in him, but it is the mystery of the spirit brought down and put to the service of men." [p. 28]

17. Letter to Mrs. O. H. Browning, April 1, 1838. ALs, 5 p. (Henry E. Huntington Library)

"Others have been made fools of by the girls; but this can never be with truth said of me — I most emphatically, in this instance, made a fool of myself."

The rejected suitor at age twenty-nine laughs at himself in a letter written on All Fools' Day.

. . . .

18. Letter to Joshua F. Speed, July 4, 1842. ALs, 3 p. (Illinois State Historical Library)

"I always was superstitious; and as part of my superstition, I believe God made me one of the instruments of bringing your Fanny [Mrs. Speed] and you together, which union, I have no doubt He had fore-ordained. Whatever he designs, he will do for *me* yet."

At age thirty-three Lincoln writes to his closest friend about girls and God.

. . . .

19. Letter to Cadet Quintin Campbell, June 28, 1862. ALs, 1 p. (Minnesota Historical Society)

"Take the advice of a friend, who, though he never saw you, deeply sympathizes with you, and stick to your purpose."

The President encourages the son of his wife's cousin to persevere at West Point.

---

[1] Abbreviations used in this section are D, document; AD, autograph document; ADs, autograph document signed; Ds, document signed; ADfs, autograph document facsimile signed; Ls, letter signed; ALs, autograph letter signed.

20. Letter to James H. Hackett, November 2, 1863. ALs, 1 p. (Mr. Alfred W. Stern, Chicago)

"I have endured a great deal of ridicule without much malice, and I have received a great deal of kindness, not quite free from ridicule."

An earlier letter to this Shakespearean actor on Lincoln's likes and dislikes in the theater had reached the newspapers. In response to an apology from the actor, the President observed that he had been used to both ridicule and kindness.

. . . .

21. Letter to Albert G. Hodges, April 4, 1864. ADfs, 3 p. (Library of Congress)

"In telling this tale I attempt no compliment to my own sagacity. I claim not to have controlled events, but confess plainly that events have controlled me. Now, at the end of three years struggle the nation's condition is not what either party, or any man devised, or expected. God alone can claim it."

The President admits to a Kentucky editor that the policies of the Government have not been determined by its Chief Executive.

III. The Thinker

Students of Lincoln agree with his friend Noah Brooks that "he was acute rather than profound." He espoused no system of philosophy, and attempts to describe his beliefs seem barren because Lincoln's thought found strength in his emotions. His mind, as an instrument for logical reasoning, was second to none.

22. Brooks, Noah, *Washington in Lincoln's Time*. New York: Century, 1895. 328 p.

"Perhaps his exceeding plainness of speech detracted somewhat from the real depth of his thought, but he was acute rather than profound; and I am inclined to think that those who were nearest him during the last years of his life were impressed by the swiftness and correctness of his intuitions, rather than by the originality and profundity of his reasoning. Some of the more radical members of his party were impatient with his "exasperating slowness"; but I never heard anyone criticize him for lack of speed in arriving at a rational conclusion when he had once undertaken an argument on any subject whatever." [p. 303]

· · · · · · · ·

23. Pargellis, Stanley, "Lincoln's Political Philosophy," *The Abraham Lincoln Quarterly*, III (June, 1945), pp. 275-290.

"The political philosophy of which these four beliefs — in expediency, in the organic nation, in a guiding idea behind it, and in God's directing Providence — constitute the basic pillars is by no means peculiar to Lincoln." [p. 287]

"And yet no one who labels Lincoln conservative can deny that this was a conservatism of a special brand. There was a dynamic, an explosive element in it, as there is in the country which has recognized in him the most sympathetic interpreter of its character and its hopes. That dynamic element is the central guiding *idea* behind the Union, the idea of the equality of men." [p. 288]

24. Randall, James G., *Lincoln, the Liberal Statesman.*
New York: Dodd, Mead, 1947. 266 p.

"It would not be going far wrong to say that the
liberal credo was the key to Lincoln's views of man
and state. His basic ideas were those of Thomas Jefferson. He owed little to Hamilton who wanted a
government to please the moneyed interests. Human
rights meant more to him than profits. He was not
content with lip service to the Declaration of Independence. He took its doctrines seriously in their
stress upon equality of men." [p. 179]

. . . .

25. Williams, T. Harry, "Abraham Lincoln — Principle
and Pragmatism in Politics: a Review Article,"
The Mississippi Valley Historical Review, XL
(June, 1953), pp. 89-106.

"There were four fundamental principles in Lincoln's
thought. These principles were the common beliefs of
most Americans in the middle period of our history.
. . . The first principle was a conviction that a Guiding Providence or some supernatural force largely
directed the affairs of men. . . . The second principle
was a concept of human nature. The men of Lincoln's
time believed that man had a higher nature. . . . The
third principle dealt with the economic activities of
man and the relationship of those activities to the
general welfare. . . . The way to property must be
open to all. . . . The fourth principle was an exaltation of the idea of the American Union. . . . By the
mere force of its example America would bring democracy to an undemocratic world." [p. 97]

26. Thomas, Benjamin P., "Abe Lincoln, Country
Lawyer," *The Atlantic Monthly,* 193 (February,
1954), pp. 57-61.

"Throughout the war, in state papers, in conversa-
tions, in private letters, in informal talks to soldiers,
he restated this idea in variant words. Identifying the
fate of the Union with the fate of the world democracy, he defined the cause of the nation in terms of
human betterment throughout the world. . . .

"A nearer realization of the American dream became
the aim of Lincoln's life. Yet he was no mere dreamer.
He realized that the struggle of human freedom is
eternal; he had no illusions of its ending in his lifetime
or in ours. He understood that the antagonisms between man's better nature and his selfishness endure,
and that it would be the fate of every generation of
Americans to defend democracy from its enemies of
greed, intolerance and despotism." [p. 61]

. . . .

DOCUMENTS

27. "Fragment on Government," [July 1, 1854] AD,
1 p. (Library of Congress)

"The legitimate object of government, is to do for a
community of people, whatever they need to have
done, but can not do, *at all,* or can not, *so well do,* for
themselves — in their separate, and individual capac-
ities."

*The mature Lincoln weighed ideas by putting them in
his own words in private memoranda.*

. . . .

28. "Definition of Democracy," [August 1, 1858] AD,

1 p. (Facsimile in the Illinois State Historical Library)

"As I would not be a *slave,* so I would not be a *master.* This expresses my idea of democracy. Whatever differs from this, to the extent of the difference, is no democracy."

. . . .

29. "Speech in Independence Hall, Philadelphia, Pennsylvania," February 22, 1861, in *The Collected Works of Abraham Lincoln.* Edited by Roy P. Basler. (New Brunswick: Rutgers University Press, 1953.) IV, pp. 240-241.

"I have often inquired of myself, what great principle or idea it was that kept this Confederacy so long together. . . . It was that which gave promise that in due time the weights should be lifted from the shoulders of all men, and that *all* should have an equal chance."

On the way to Washington for his first inauguration, President-Elect Lincoln is moved to speak on the significance of the Declaration of Independence.

. . . .

30. Letter to Horace Greeley, August 22, 1862. ALs, 3 p. (Wadsworth Athenaeum, Hartford, Connecticut)

"My paramount object in this struggle *is* to save the Union, and is *not* either to save or to destroy slavery."

The President settles a troublesome editor.

. . . .

31. "Meditation on the Divine Will," [September 2, 1862] AD, 1 p. (Illinois State Historical Library)

"The will of God prevails. In great contests each
party claims to act in accordance with the will of God.
Both *may* be, and one *must* be wrong. God can not be
for, and *against* the same thing at the same time."

*The logical mind of the President considers the role of
the Ruler of Nations in the American Civil War.*

IV. *The Statesman*

As President, Lincoln was a statesman of surpassing skill.
His successes in relations with members of his cabinet,
military leaders, congressmen, journalists, and with common people in all walks of life depended on years of growth
and seasoning as a politician in Illinois. An activity involving countless incidents which occurred throughout most of
a lifetime cannot be fairly represented in an exhibit; the
books and documents shown here provide but a minute
glimpse of Lincoln's major vocation — politics.

. . . .

32. Randall, James G., "Lincoln and the Governance
of Men," *The Abraham Lincoln Quarterly,* VI
(June, 1951), pp. 327-352.

"With Lincoln the technique of public relations was
closely bound up with the art of human relations. In
personal dealings Lincoln put a new meaning into the
word 'tact.' He could maintain poise, avoid awkward
'showdown,' and steer the conversation. In his presence embarrassment disappeared, courtesy was raised
to an exquisite level, and a touch of human interest
was added to the passing moment or the everyday
routine." [p. 331]

33. Williams, T. Harry, *Lincoln and His Generals*. New York: Knopf, 1952. 363 p.

"With no knowledge of the theory of war, no experience in war, and no technical training, Lincoln, by the power of his mind, became a fine strategist. He was a better natural strategist than were most of the trained soldiers. He saw the big picture of the war from the start. . . . He grasped immediately the advantage that numbers gave the North and urged his generals to keep up a constant pressure on the whole strategic line of the Confederacy until a weak spot was found — and a break-through could be made. And he soon realized, if he did not know it at the beginning, that the proper objective of his armies was the destruction of the Confederate armies and not the occupation of Southern territory." [p. 7]

. . . .

34. Thomas, Benjamin P., *Abraham Lincoln, a Biography*. New York: Knopf, 1952. 548 p.

"Tough, shrewd, and canny in his younger years, the man who was bringing the nation through to victory had become strong, merciful, and wise. Success had come to him, and to the nation that he served, because he had lived and governed according to its ideals." [p. 498]

. . . .

35. Horner, Harlan Hoyt, *Lincoln and Greeley*. [Urbana] University of Illinois Press, 1953. 432 p.

"Myths about Lincoln as being different from other men are dispelled by the record of Lincoln, the consummate politician. Other presidents have sought re-election more openly, directly, and frankly, but none has quite equaled the political artistry of Abraham Lincoln." [p. 357]

Copy inscribed by the author "For the Lincoln Room with the hope that down through the years it will be increasingly useful to students of Lincoln's life and time."

. . . .

36. Donald, David, "Abraham Lincoln and the American Pragmatic Tradition," in *Lincoln Reconsidered, Essays on the Civil War Era.* (New York: Knopf, 1956.) Pp. 128-143.

"As a statesman, he was leader in a democratic society, and he firmly believed that such a free government represented 'the last, best hope of earth.' He knew that the successful democratic leader must not be too far ahead of his following." [p. 142]

. . . .

DOCUMENTS

37. "Communication to the People of Sangamo County," Springfield *Sangamo Journal,* March 15, 1832, p. 1.

"My case is thrown exclusively upon the independent voters of this county, and if elected they will have conferred a favor upon me, for which I shall be unremitting in my labors to compensate. But if the good people in their wisdom shall see fit to keep me in the background, I have been too familiar with disappointments to be very much chagrined."

At age twenty-three Lincoln appeals to the voters of his county for their support in his candidacy for election to the state legislature. He lost the election, but of the 300 votes cast in the New Salem precinct, Lincoln received 277.

· · · · · · · · ·

38. Letter to Owen Lovejoy, August 11, 1855. ALs, 3 p. (Henry E. Huntington Library)

"Not even *you* are more anxious to prevent the extension of slavery than I; and yet the political atmosphere is such, just now, that I fear to do anything, lest I do wrong."

Although the Whig Party was moribund, Lincoln was unwilling in 1855 to join the new Republican Party because he did not wish to take "an open stand" against "old political and personal friends."

· · · · · · · · ·

39. Letter to Henry Asbury, November 19, 1858. ALs, 1 p.

"The fight must go on. The cause of civil liberty must not be surrendered at the end of *one,* or even, one *hundred* defeats."

A defeated candidate for the United States Senate looks to the future.

· · · · · · · · ·

40. Letter to Horatio Seymour, March 23, 1863. ALs, 1 p. (Facsimile in the Illinois State Historical Library)

"In the performance of my duty, the cooperation of your State, as that of others, is needed — in fact, is indispensable. This alone is a sufficient reason why I should wish to be at a good understanding with you."

The President makes a gesture of friendship to the new Democratic Governor of New York.

41. "Response to a Serenade," November 10, 1864. AD, 4 p. (Southworth Library, Dryden, New York)

"But the rebellion continues; and now that the election is over, may not all, having a common interest, re-unite in a common effort, to save our common country? For my own part I have striven, and shall strive to avoid placing any obstacle in the way. So long as I have been here I have not willingly planted a thorn in any man's bosom."

The President acknowledges congratulations on his re-election and appeals to men of both parties to make a concerted effort to win the War.

V. *The Artist*

"The Enduring Lincoln" stands forth in his writings in which he often achieved a rare artistry. Of the many efforts to explain Lincoln's style, probably the most successful is Mark Van Doren's: "The secret was simple, perhaps. Lincoln thought and felt every word he wrote. . . . The depth of Lincoln's thought was one with the depth of his feeling; after which, no doubt, his style took care of itself." (New York *Herald Tribune Book Review,* February 8, 1953, p. 6.)

. . . .

42. Angle, Paul M., "Lincoln's Power with Words," in *Abraham Lincoln Association Papers.* (Springfield: Abraham Lincoln Association, 1935.) Pp. 59-87.

"Measured by many standards, Abraham Lincoln was a master of words. In his writings fuse sincerity and sympathy, logical directness, a severity of style almost classic, and homely plainness. Yet these attributes in themselves fail to explain the attraction of his writings. It is because his own great qualities — his ruggedness, his tenderness, his tolerance, his humility — are mirrored in what he wrote that his words will live as long as the English tongue." [p. 87]

. . . .

43. Basler, Roy P., "Abraham Lincoln — Artist," *North American Review*, 245 (Spring, 1938), pp. 144-153.

"Lincoln was above all an artist, and though his art was far from confined to literary expression, his prose may yet be recognized as his most permanent legacy to humanity." [p. 144]

. . . .

44. Basler, Roy P., "Abraham Lincoln's Rhetoric," *American Literature*, XI (May, 1939), pp. 167-182.

"Repetition, grammatical parallelism, and antithesis may be considered the most obvious technical devices of Lincoln's general style. He uses these devices with such frequency and variety of effect that it seems to have been a consistent habit of his mind to seek repetitive sequences in both diction and sentence structure for the alignment of his thought." [p. 167]

. . . .

45. Nevins, Allan, "Lincoln in His Writings," in *The Life and Writings of Abraham Lincoln*. Edited by Philip Van Doren Stern. (New York: Random House [c1940].) Pp. xvii-xxvi

"A study of Lincoln's writings obviously has two great elements of interest, one historical, the other

biographical. . . . Most men will read Lincoln either
to find out what contributions he was making to his
time, or to learn something about his mind, heart and
personality. And of these two elements, the historical
and the biographical, the latter is by far the more
alluring and important." [pp. xvii-xviii]

. . . .

46. Basler, Roy P., "Lincoln's Development as a
    Writer," in *Abraham Lincoln: His Speeches and
    Writings*. Edited by Roy P. Basler. (Cleveland:
    World [c1946].) Pp. 1-49.

"The study of Lincoln's works reveals the dignity of
a great mind and heart that seeks for rightness in
principle, fairness in act, and beauty in utterance.
. . . Time may dissipate the factual significance of
his deeds, both as private citizen and as President, but
we must always know and acknowledge the shining
spirit that illumines his words." [pp. 48-49]

. . . .

47. Blegen, Theodore C., *Lincoln's Imagery, a Study in
    Word Power*. La Crosse: Sumac Press, 1954. 32 p.

"No single facet of the mind of Lincoln can explain
the man and his role in his own day — and his enduring fame. It is the whole man, in the amplitude of his
mind and character, who met greatly the crisis of civil
war and who lives greatly in the memory of America
and the world. But we can help turn the legend of
Lincoln into the living reality of the man by looking
at the words with which he clothed his thought and
conviction." [p. 31]

DOCUMENTS

48. *"A House Divided Against Itself Cannot Stand."* Introduction by Douglas C. McMurtrie. Chicago: Black Cat Press, 1936. 29 p.

"The result is not doubtful. We shall not fail — if we stand firm, we shall not fail.

"Wise counsels may accelerate or mistakes delay it, but, sooner or later, the victory is sure to come." [p. 29]

The leader of the Republicans of Illinois speaks with a new voice.

. . . .

49. "Farewell Address at Springfield," February 11, 1861. AD, 1 p. (Library of Congress)

"No one, not in my situation, can appreciate my feeling of sadness at this parting. To this place, and the kindness of these people, I owe everything."

The President-Elect speaks to his neighbors who had gathered in the Springfield railroad station to say goodbye on his departure for Washington.

The speech was written in pencil as the train left Springfield. The first nine lines are in Lincoln's hand; the remainder were dictated by Lincoln to secretary John G. Nicolay.

. . . .

50. *The Address . . . Delivered at Cooper Institute, February 27th, 1860.* With Notes by Charles C. Nott & Cephas Brainerd. New York: George F. Nesbitt, 1860. 32 p.

"Neither let us be slandered from our duty by false accusations against us, nor frightened from it by menaces of destruction to the Government nor of dungeons to ourselves. LET US HAVE FAITH THAT RIGHT MAKES MIGHT, AND IN THAT FAITH, LET US, TO THE END, DARE TO DO OUR DUTY AS WE UNDERSTAND IT." [p. 32]

A candidate for the Republican nomination for President in 1860 makes his bid for Eastern support.

. . . .

51. "Annual Message to Congress," December 1, 1862. Ds, 86 p. (The National Archives)

"Fellow-citizens, *we* cannot escape history. . . . The fiery trial through which we pass will light us down, in honor or dishonor, to the latest generation. . . . We shall nobly save, or meanly lose, the last best, hope of earth." [p. 85]

The President makes an eloquent (and unsuccessful) plea to Congress to endorse his plan for compensated emancipation of slaves.

. . . .

52. Letter to Fanny McCullough, December 23, 1862. ALs, 1 p. (Miss Alice Orme Smith, Fairfield, Connecticut)

"In this sad world of ours, sorrow comes to all; and, to the young, it comes with bitterest agony, because it takes them unawares. The older have learned to ever expect it."

The President comforts the daughter of a sometime clerk of an Illinois court who had been killed in battle.

. . . .

53. Letter to Joseph Hooker, January 26, 1863. ALs, 2 p. (Mr. Alfred W. Stern, Chicago)

"I have placed you at the head of the Army of the Potomac. Of course I have done this upon what appears to me to be sufficient reasons. And yet I think it best for you to know that there are some things in regard to which, I am not quite satisfied with you."

The President states his misgivings to the general he has elevated.

VI. *The President's Vision*

"The Enduring Lincoln" is greater than the sum of its parts. In his finest moments, President Lincoln spoke for people everywhere.

. . . .

54. Nevins, Allan, "Lincoln as More Than a Statesman," in *The Statesmanship of the Civil War*. The Page-Barbour Lectures, University of Virginia, 1951. (New York: Macmillan, 1953.) Pp. 57-82.

"A supreme realist, in one respect he was often ready to abandon realism. That is, he was ready, on fit occasion, to appeal to a spirit of idealism and generosity which hardly existed — which was almost imperceptible — but which his appeal could sometimes call into being; a coal of finer feeling which his example and his simple eloquence could sometimes fan into flame. We have said that he almost always addressed himself to men who differed from him, not to friends, and that he appealed to their reason, not their prejudices and emotions. He did more than this: he appealed to their better selves. And his appeal to the country at large was an appeal to its nobler side, its better nature." [p. 79]

DOCUMENTS

55. "First Inaugural Address," March 4, 1861. D and AD. (Library of Congress)

"Though passion may have strained it must not break our bonds of affection. The mystic chords of memory, stretching from every battle-field, and patriot grave, to every living heart and hearthstone, all over this broad land, will yet swell the chorus of the Union, when again touched, as surely they will be, by the better angels of our nature."

The new President makes an emotional appeal to the South.

. . . .

56. "War Message to Congress," July 4, 1861. AD. (Library of Congress)

"This is essentially a people's contest. On the side of the Union, it is a struggle for maintaining in the world, that form, and substance of government, whose leading object is to elevate the condition of men — to lift artificial weights from all shoulders — to clear the paths of laudable pursuit for all — to afford all an unfettered start, and a fair chance, in the race of life. Yielding to partial, and temporary departures, from necessity, this is the leading object of the government for whose existence we contend."

. . . .

57. Letter to James C. Conkling, August 26, 1863. Ls, 8 p. (Illinois State Historical Library)

"The signs look better. The Father of Waters again goes unvexed to the sea. . . . Thanks to all. For the great republic — for the principle it lives by, and keeps alive — for man's vast future, — thanks to all."

*This letter was copied from Lincoln's final draft by a
clerk.*

. . . .

58. "Address Delivered at the Dedication of the Ceme-
tery at Gettysburg," November 19, 1863. ADs, 3 p.
(Mr. Oscar Cintas, Havana, Cuba)

"It is rather for us to be here dedicated to the great
task remaining before us — . . . that government of
the people, by the people, for the people, shall not
perish from the earth."

*This is the last of the five versions of the Address at
Gettysburg in Lincoln's hand.*

. . . .

59. "Second Inaugural Address," March 4, 1865. AD,
4 p. (Library of Congress)

". . . let us strive on to finish the work we are in;
. . . to do all which may achieve and cherish a just,
and a lasting peace, among ourselves, and with all
nations."

INDEX